To. Bill White,

The Power is Yours

David Ramiah

All scriptures are taken from the authorized King James Version "KJV"
of the Bible unless otherwise noted.

*Let the power
of Christ
manifest
through you
more & more !
Pastor David.*

1

"Your future is not dependent on your past. It depends on what you believe in your heart."

"For as he thinks in his heart, so is he." Proverbs 23:7
NKJV

The Power is Yours
Edited by: Ingrid Nasagar and Mr. Fred "Frits" Bax
Final Edit: Mrs Joy Hallwood

Published in Canada
Revised Edition
ISBN 978-0-9733247-6-1

Rev. David Ramiah
910 Eglinton Ave., E.,
Mississauga, Ontario, L4W 1K1
www.LivingAboveAndBeyond.com

Printed in the USA – 2008

Dedication

I dedicate this book to my
Lord and Saviour Jesus Christ.

Acknowledgement

*This book is written in memory of **Peter Melic** who was like a father to me and a very close friend. Peter helped fashion and mould countless numbers of lives by his Christian life and teaching. He will always be remembered.*

*It is also written in honor of **Jacobus Mooij** who was also like a father to me. His dedication to the Lord is to be admired, and his leadership quality is an example to follow.*

To my Mom and Dad: thank you for your love and support without which I wouldn't be doing what I do. I love you both very much.

To three guys and one gal who makes life a joy: my nephews and my niece; Ryan, Jonathan, Joshua and Briana. I love you!

To my sisters, my brothers and my two sister-in-laws: your love and confidence in me has supported me all the way. I love you. God bless all of you.

To Grandma Liz: there is no one else like you. I love you!

Special thanks to:

Fred Bax
Dorra Bellamy
Miriam Canon
Lou Cianfarani
Padre Steve and Norma Heemskerk
Ingrid Nasagar
Rev. John McDonald
Rev. Douglas Rowley
Angie Seruga
Karlene Spence
Stephen Stelmach

Contents

Introduction

People everywhere are suffering one kind of hurt or another. And many are frustrated, confused and angry. They do not know where to turn, who to go to, or what to do. They are dismayed, have lost hope and may not have the motivation to go on.

What to do? How to get out of situations? Solve problems? Where are the answers? How do I make it? Where do I go?

Human beings have an enemy who has plagued them for ages. Suffering and groaning for generations under the strain, humans have bent low to the gruelling weight of his torment. But, he will not torment us for much longer. His time is short!

There is a bright and glorious day ahead of us. That day will dawn on us very soon. And when it does, we shall have great joy and gladness of heart. For Satan, that enemy of both mankind and God will be cast into the Lake of Everlasting Fire, where he and his host shall burn forever.

We will have joy and we shall have peace. However, until then we still have to face this enemy on a daily basis.

But, there is great hope! For we do not face him alone, but we come against him covered with the blood of

Jesus Christ. And we overcome him by the blood of Jesus and the word of our testimony. We defeat him in the name of Jesus Christ our Lord and Savior!

One day you will be able to say, "I overcame him in the area of finances. I overcame him in my business, in my marriage, and on my children's behalf. I defeated him in the name of Jesus Christ every step of the way."

The enemy is a defeated foe! Christ Jesus defeated him two thousand years ago, when He died on the cross and rose again from the dead. Today, you must apply that to your life. You need to live in that on a daily basis by acknowledging this truth and confessing it in your life.

When the devil comes against you in temptation and struggles, you have to rebuke him in the name of Jesus Christ. He will flee from you! If he tries to bring strife and division in your family, you will break and destroy his influence on your family in Christ's name. You will overcome him if he tries to destroy your business or steal your finances. You will defeat him every which way he may try to get you. Because Jesus Christ has given you power to overcome.

You therefore must learn to know your enemy. Understand how he operates and in what way he moves against people. You will also need to know how to defeat him. And for that, you must read on!

"Be sober, be vigilant; because your adversary the devil, as a roaring lion, walketh about, seeking whom he may devour." 1st Peter 5: 8

Chapter One

The Garden Experience

Six thousand years ago, a most dramatic event took place in the Garden of Eden that would influence every future event. This occurrence was not only remarkable, but was unique and entirely supernatural. It was the creation of man and his wife.

To understand our existence as a race; to know where we are going and to know the power and the ability that lies on the inside of us, we must return to the Garden. When we comprehend the great significance of this major occasion in Eden, we will then be able to envision the bigger picture.

The Spirit of God moved upon the face of the deep. He brooded and waited and then He said,

"Let us make man in our image, after our likeness and let them have dominion over the fish of the sea and over the fowl of the air, and over the cattle and over all the earth and over every creeping thing that creepeth upon the earth." And so God created man in His own image, in the image of God created He him, male and female created He them. And God blessed them and God said unto them, "be fruitful

*and multiply and replenish the earth, and subdue it,
and have dominion over the fowl of the air and over
every living thing that moveth upon the earth."
Genesis 1:26 – 28*

God created the heavens above and the earth
beneath. He made the animals, the sea, the oceans, the fish,
the birds, the bees, the trees, the sun, the moon and the
stars. The Lord saw everything that He had created and said
it was good.

God Almighty made mankind in His own image and
likeness. They were placed in the Garden of Eden and *were
given power to rule the earth* and everything in it. When
the Lord made man, He made Him with a plan and purpose.
And the Lord was specific with His plan and purpose: make
man in God's likeness and image and give him power to
rule the earth.

*"And the Lord God formed man of the dust of the
ground and breathed into his nostrils the breath of
life, and man became a living soul. And the Lord
God said, "It is not good that the man should be
alone, I will make a help meet (mate) for him." And
the Lord God caused a deep sleep to fall upon
Adam and he slept, and he took one of his ribs and
closed up the flesh instead thereof. And the rib
which the Lord God had taken from man, made He
a woman, and brought her unto the man. And Adam
said, "This is now bone of my bones, and flesh of
my flesh, she shall be called woman because she
was taken out of man. Therefore, shall a man leave
his father and his mother and shall cleave unto his
wife and they shall be one flesh."
Genesis 2:7, 18, 21-24*

God our Creator literally molded man into shape just as a potter molds clay into a pot. Taking the dust of the ground He formed the man. Then He created the soul and spirit by breathing them into man.

We could imagine that God was sitting on the ground when He created Adam. With His own hands He gathered the dust of the ground together. Then as a potter would do, He molded the dust (mud) into the shape of man. After the man was molded into his physical form, the Lord, bending over, breathed into the man's nostrils. The man became a living being.

Imagine the man. He is alive. He looked up and saw his Father - God. Perhaps he said "Hi Father." And God said, "Hi Son, you look good."

Later Adam gave names to all the animals, and God saw that he was alone and said: "It is not good for the man to be alone." Genesis 2:18

He then made a woman for the man. She was to be his help-meet (mate). She would meet him emotionally, spiritually, physically and intellectually. She would be his counterpart.

Adam was placed in a deep sleep and God took a rib out of his side. His flesh was then healed. Taking the rib that He had taken from the man, God created Eve. In creating the woman, God *skillfully formed* her and then brought her to Adam.

Adam saw Eve. And I do not believe for a minute that He just laid there trying to wake up. He must have jumped up to his feet and said: *"Father, you said I looked good! She's gorgeous!"*

I believe Eve was the most beautiful woman that ever walked the earth. Remember, she is the mother of us all.

15

God gave Eve to Adam to be his wife, and Adam said:

"This is now bone of my bones and flesh of my flesh. She shall be called woman." Genesis 1:24

The man and the woman became one. There union was now complete. They became one flesh.

~ One Flesh ~

The Bible tells us that the man and his wife became one flesh. Did they become one flesh when God brought Eve to Adam? Or was it at some point after their union? When did they become one flesh?

"Therefore shall a man leave his father and his mother, and shall cleave unto his wife and they shall be one flesh." Genesis 2:24

This clearly shows us that it was after a man left his mother and father and clung to his wife! It was after marriage and the consummation of the marriage that they became *one flesh*. Therefore it was after Adam and Eve came together as husband and wife that this union took place.

When God brought Eve to Adam, Adam said;

"This is now bone of my bones and flesh of my flesh." Genesis 2:23

He said that because he knew God had taken a rib out of him and made Eve. Adam was wise. God made him that way. He had to be wise to rule this earth as God had commanded him. He fellowshipped and walked with God daily, learning from Him. (Genesis 3: 8)

When the man looked upon his wife he saw himself in her. Adam saw himself in Eve. She was his flesh and blood, his bone, his very body.

Becoming one flesh is a great mystery. However, if we were to take the Bible literally for what it says, we would understand enough of this mystery to apply it to our lives.

The rib that God took from Adam was taken out for a purpose. It was made into a beautiful, living, creative being that he called "woman".

God could have created Eve just the same way He had created Adam, using just the dust of the ground, but He didn't. *He had a better plan!*

~ Youthful Longing ~

Most single people at a certain age desire to be joined together in marriage.

When a man and a woman are married, and their marriage is consummated through sexual intercourse, one of the world's greatest mysteries takes place. They become one flesh. The rib that was taken from man and was made into a woman is reunited to the man.

> *"Know ye not that your bodies are the members of Christ? Shall I then take the members of Christ, and make them the members of an harlot? God forbid. What? Know ye not that he which is joined to an harlot is one body? For two, saith he, shall be one flesh." 1st Corinthians 6: 15-16*

> *"Wherefore they are no more twain, but one flesh. What therefore God hath joined together, let no man put asunder." Matthew 19:6*

17

You must understand that God did not have to take a rib from Adam to make Eve. He could have formed her from the dust of the ground just like he did Adam. He took that rib out of Adam for a purpose. And the purpose is that a man would long for his rib that is alive, the woman who belongs to him. At the same time the rib which is alive, the woman, would long to be joined back to the body from which she came.

Sure, there is sexual longing, but this is not what I am talking about. This is a more intense longing that comes from deep within a person, from his innermost being. It is a longing of acceptance and completeness.

When that rib is reunited to the body from which it came -*the woman to the man* in holy matrimony, there is completeness. They are one. The deep longing subsides and gives place to love and harmony, joy and peace of mind. The rib is united back with the body and the body is complete again.

People often ask me these questions: "Why do I still long for him? Why do I still yearn for her? Why can't I just get on with my life?"

The answer is this: you are one flesh with that person; you belong together. For a woman, it is your body - the man that you came from. For the man, it is your rib - the woman who is out there, needing to reunite with him.

To become one flesh the rib must be joined back to the body it came from.

Imagine a man on an operating table. The doctor comes in, opens up his side and takes a rib out of him. He walks over to another table with the rib and prepares it. After he is finished preparing the rib, he takes it and puts it back into the man's side. He then stitches up the wound. The man is complete again.

This is what happens when two people are married and their marriage is consummated. They become one flesh. They are fully united together as one.

~ The Fall of Mankind ~

"Be fruitful and multiply." This was a command by the Lord to Adam and Eve. After God created the man and the woman, He gave them this command. They were to be fruitful, multiply and replenish the earth. And they were to subdue it by having dominion over the fish of the sea, over the birds of the air, and over every living thing that was in it.

In essence, man was given power from God to rule the earth and everything in it.

God also planted a garden –Eden, where He placed the man and his wife Eve. He told him to "dress it" and "keep it". Read *Genesis Chapter 2*.

The Hebrew word "*shamar*" where we get the word "*keep*" from, means to hedge about, guard or protect. When we recognize the fact that there was a need to protect the garden, we realize that man and God must have had an enemy. This was the same enemy who caused the fall of man.

Two significant trees were planted in the Garden of Eden by the Lord God. They were; the Tree of Life and the Tree of the Knowledge of Good and Evil. God had said to the man not to eat from the Tree of the Knowledge of Good and Evil. The Lord told him that if he did, he would surely die.

"And the Lord God planted a garden eastward in Eden, and there he put the man whom he had formed. And out of the ground made the Lord God to grow every tree that is pleasant to the sight, and good for food, the Tree of Life also in the midst of the Garden, and the Tree of the Knowledge of Good and Evil, and the Lord God took the man and put him into the Garden of Eden to dress it and to keep it... and the Lord God commanded the man, saying, of every tree of the Garden thou mayest freely eat. But of the Tree of the Knowledge of good and evil, thou shalt not eat of it, for in the day that thou eatest thereof thou shalt surely die."
Genesis 2:8, 9, 15-17

Adam and his wife Eve directly disobeyed the Lord after He had told them not to eat from the Tree of the Knowledge of Good and Evil. They ate from the tree after they were tempted, and because of that they fell from the grace of God.

Adam did not have to think about eating from that particular tree. He already knew that he shouldn't eat of the fruit of it. God had specifically told him not to.

"The serpent was more subtle than any beast of the field which the Lord God had made, and he said unto the woman, yea, hath God said, you shall not eat of every tree of the Garden? And the woman said unto the serpent, we may eat of the fruit of the trees of the Garden. But of the fruit of the tree which is in the midst of the Garden, God hath said, ye shall not eat of it, neither shall ye touch it, lest ye die. And the serpent said unto the woman, ye shall not surely die. For God doth know that in the day ye eat thereof, then your eyes shall be opened, and ye shall be as gods, knowing good and evil, and when

the woman saw that the tree was good for food, and that it was pleasant to the eyes, and a tree to be desired to make one wise, she took of the fruit thereof, and did eat, and gave also unto her husband with her and he did eat, and the eyes of them both were opened, and they knew that they were naked, and they sewed fig leaves together and made themselves aprons." Genesis 3:1-7

Before man sinned he had no shame and did not recognize that he was naked and needed to be covered. This was because he was covered with the glory of God. Adam and Eve did not need a covering. They were pure and holy. God was their covering.

When they ate of the fruit however, they obtained knowledge of good and evil and realized that they were naked. And this is because the glory of God had been removed from them.

"And the eyes of them both were opened and they knew that they were naked, and they sewed fig leaves together and made themselves aprons." Genesis 3:7

So their eyes were opened. They saw differently. They realized that they had sinned and were guilty, so they hid themselves. We see this in the following verse from Genesis:

"And they heard the voice of the Lord God walking in the cool of the day, and Adam and his wife hid themselves from the presence of the Lord God amongst the trees of the Garden." Genesis 3:8

~ The Serpent's Bite ~

Adam and his wife were tempted and they succumbed to temptation. The devil used the most cunning beast to do his dirty work for him. After he had agreed with the serpent on the most effective way of causing the fall of man, they went into action. They were definitely partners in this plot against man.

> *"And the Lord God said unto the serpent, because thou hast done this, thou art cursed above all cattle and above every beast of the field, upon thy belly shalt thou go, and dust shalt thou eat all the days of thy life. And I will put enmity between thee and the woman, and between thy seed and her seed it shall bruise thy head, and thou shall bruise his heel."*
> *Genesis 3:14, 15*

Speaking directly to the serpent, God put a curse on him. He decreed that the serpent would crawl on his belly and eat the dust of the ground. This was the punishment for his part in the fall of man.

You need to understand that God would not have put a curse upon the serpent for no reason. He is just and judges righteously. The serpent had to have had a part in the fall of man. He had to have been Satan's partner. And he was.

The devil told the man and woman that they would be as gods if they ate from the fruit of the tree. They would know good and evil.

Well, they now knew good and evil, but they had not become like God. Instead they had become like the devil. They had lost all that had been given to them by God. By separating themselves from the Lord and joining themselves to the devil, they became like the devil. Now they share in sin, fear, guilt, shame, and the loss of godliness. They were separated from God -spiritual death. They now shared the nature of Satan!

Some believe that the devil took the form of a serpent, but it was not so. If it was anything, it would be a possession of the serpent by the devil. Thus he used it to do his dirty work. Satan has the ability to possess or demonize; entering into and having control of a creature.

However, there was a partnership between them. And the serpent received the punishment due him because of his cooperation.

I believe that the devil used the serpent because he was not allowed to enter the garden. But, the serpent was allowed to go in and out.

God had told Adam and Eve that if they ate from the tree of the knowledge of good and evil they would die. And they died, immediately! They did not die physically, but spiritually. Physical death came later. (*Genesis 3:19*).

Before sin came upon man he had a divine connection with God. Adam and Eve were pure, holy and innocent. God is pure and holy, and innocent of sin. God and man were in harmony and they were united. They were one in holiness.

Sin, however, came into this world through the disobedience of Adam and Eve. And because of their sin, mankind has since been separated spiritually from God.

~ Broken Relationship ~

The man and the woman took on a sinful nature after they sinned. The oneness between them and God was broken. God cannot and will not be joined to sin.

Four things happened immediately after Adam and Eve sinned:
1) Sin came into man;
2) Man was separated spiritually from God -spiritual death;
3) Physical death came upon man; and
4) The devil stole from Adam, the power to rule the earth.

Adam had power and authority to rule the earth. This authority was given to him by God, but he lost it to the devil when he sinned. Through disobedience man sinned, and became sin.

Today, when a child is born, he is born in sin because of his forefather, Adam. Sin therefore passed from generation to generation. The Word of God attests to this in Romans 3:23

"For all have sinned and come short of the glory of God."

You will find a picture of a man born in sin in *John 9:34.* This is what it says: "They answered and said unto him, thou wast altogether born in sins, and dost thou teach us? And they cast him out."

From this passage it can clearly be seen that we have inherited a sinful nature. Man died spiritually the same day that Adam and Eve disobeyed God -*Genesis 2:17*!

Physical death came into the world because of sin. It is the result of sin. It was not God's plan for man.

"In the sweat of thy face shalt thou eat bread, till thou return unto the ground, for out of it wast thou taken, for dust thou art, and unto dust shalt thou return." Genesis 3:19

Physical death is the result of sin. Man dies so that he will not continue to live forever in sin. However, God's plan was to deliver man from sin, redeeming him to Himself.

In *Genesis 1:26 and 28*, we see that God had given all authority to man to rule the earth. But when they sinned and were separated from God, they literally put themselves into the hands of the devil. Satan then stole this power to rule from them because Adam had become the servant of the devil. From that time on, the devil began to rule the earth.

"Know ye not, that to whom ye yield yourselves servants to obey, his servants ye are to whom ye obey, whether of sin unto death, or of obedience unto righteousness?" Romans 6:16

"Now is the judgement of this world: Now shall the prince of this world be cast out." John 12: 31

"....for the prince of this world cometh, and hath nothing in me." John 14:30

"Of judgment, because the prince of this world is judged." John 16:11

Once man fell and became the servant of the devil, the devil stole the power to rule from him, and began to govern the earth. So this is how man fell and sin came into him. He was separated spiritually from God, physical death came upon him, and the devil took control over the earth.

Chapter Two

Redemption

There have been two powers operating on the earth since the fall of Satan; the power of God and the power of the devil. Man disobeyed God and joined himself to the devil through disobedience, which is sin. This gave the devil authority to rule. Adam became his servant and he was able to tell Adam what to do. He now called the shots, *but thanks to God!* God did not leave Adam and his children helpless. He provided deliverance.

You are close to God's heart and He loves you more than you will ever be able to fully comprehend while on this earth. He made you. You are his property; His treasured possession.

The devil had stolen from God. He stole man. He thought he had outsmarted God, not realizing that he had set himself up for total destruction. The day is coming when God will cast the devil and all his demons and fallen angels into the Lake of Everlasting Fire, which will never burn out.

The Lake of Everlasting Fire was not made for man, but for Satan and his host of devils. Sadly, many who are not in Christ will find themselves there one day. There is an escape and it is through the One who paid the price for your sin. Through everlasting life in Christ, you will not have to share the Lake of Everlasting Fire with Satan.

Right after the fall of man, God's plan of redemption went into action. His plan of sending our Redeemer: Jesus Christ.

In Genesis 3:15, we see a double reference when the Lord spoke to the Serpent. He directed His speech to the serpent, but was referring to the devil. This is when He said He would put enmity between the woman and the devil, and between his seed and her seed. The same kind of reference was made when Jesus turned to Peter, but rebuked the devil *(Matthew 16.23)*.

In the previous chapter, you saw how there was a partnership between the devil and the serpent. As a partner, the serpent received the punishment due to him. Likewise, as Satan's partner, he was receiving the word for the devil. God was referring only to an invisible being who used the serpent as his tool. That invisible being was Satan.

When God said He would put enmity between Satan's seed and Eve's seed, He was referring to Jesus. Jesus is the seed of the woman.

"Therefore, the Lord himself shall give you a sign, behold a virgin shall conceive and bear a son and shall call his name Immanuel." Isaiah 7:14

"To a virgin espoused to a man, whose name was Joseph, of the house of David, and the virgin's name was Mary." Luke 1:27

And the angel said unto her, "Fear not Mary, for thou hast found favour with God. And behold thou shalt conceive in thy womb and bring forth a Son, and shalt call his name Jesus." Luke 1:30-31

Jesus is the seed of the woman who was spoken about in Genesis 3:15. His birth was foretold thousands of years by Moses before He was born, and hundreds of years before that, by Isaiah. He was born exactly as was prophesied.

Satan first tricked the woman to sin. God turned the table around and used a woman; Mary, a virgin. She brought forth the seed that would later crush the devil's head.

Mary brought forth *our Savior* into this world. He is Jesus Christ, our Redeemer, who has ransomed us from the hands of the devil. She brought forth the second Adam who was not going to fail.

The virgin birth is a mystery that is still causing skeptics and some believers alike, to ponder and debate the "whys" and "how come" of it. To this day, countless numbers of people in the world are still trying to discount the virgin birth of Jesus. And there are all kinds of "reasons" based on human intelligence and "whys" given to disbelieve His birth.

Why was Jesus born of a virgin?

"And so it is written the first man Adam was made a living soul; the last Adam was made a quickening spirit. 1st Corinthians 15:45

"For as in Adam all die, even so in Christ (last Adam), shall all be made alive." 1st Corinthians 15:22

Evidently, you see that Jesus is the second Adam. The first Adam fell and brought sin and death upon man.

The second Adam brought redemption and life. He brought freedom from sin, death and hell.

In the previous chapter we discussed how we are all born in sin because Adam is our Forefather. Jesus would have also been born in sin if Mary and Joseph were engaged in a sexual relationship. However, Jesus was placed in the womb of Mary by the Holy Spirit. Thus, He was pure and holy at his birth, just like the first Adam was before his fall.

God is the Father of Jesus, not man. Jesus came from God. He came out of God. He is God!

If Jesus had any sin in Him, He could not have been the perfect sacrifice. He was not born of man, but of God. Mary was a vessel used by God to bring Jesus into the world. *Being from God and coming out of God, Jesus had God's nature.*

> *"Now the birth of Jesus Christ was on this wise, when as his mother Mary was espoused to Joseph before they came together, she was found with child of the Holy Ghost." Matthew 1:18*

Jesus was God and is God -John 17:8. If Jesus had any sin in Him, He would not have been able to destroy Satan. Only through a perfect, pure, sinless man could redemption come. It could have only come about through the perfect sacrifice.

It was prophesied that Jesus would be born of a virgin. And He was the *"seed of the woman"* that destroyed the work of the devil.

Jesus Christ redeemed man back to God by being the perfect and ultimate sacrifice. The whole purpose of

Jesus coming to this earth was to give His life for us. He came to die for us on the cross at Calvary, and to be resurrected from the dead. In so doing, *He paid the total price for us,* which is the penalty for our sins.

"The wages of sin is death..." Romans 6:23

He also came to preach the gospel to us; the good news.

Jesus did not sin, we did. He did not deserve to die, we did. But He died, paying the price for us, redeeming us back to our Father God.

"As the Father knoweth me, even so know I the Father, and I lay down my life for the sheep" (people). John 10:15

"Therefore, doth my Father love me, because I lay down my life, that I might take it again. No man taketh it from me, but I lay it down of myself. I have power to lay it down, and I have power to take it again. This commandment have I received of my Father." John 10:17-18

Read Matthew Chapter 26 to 28 to see the death, burial and resurrection of Jesus.

At the age of twelve, Jesus was found engaged in deep discussion with scholars in the temple who were amazed at His knowledge. The display of pure wisdom was seen both in the questions He asked, and the answers He gave. His wisdom was demonstrated before all, even as a child. *(Luke 2:42 to 52)*

When our Lord was about thirty years old, He was led into the wilderness and was tempted by the devil for forty days. *(Luke 4: 1-14)* Jesus overcame the temptations of the devil.

In His life, Jesus conquered sin. And in His death and resurrection He conquered the devil totally. He did what the first Adam failed to do.

His last words on the cross were *"It is finished."* *(John 19:30).*

~ Atonement ~

After the "fall of man," men began to offer sacrifices to God for their sins.

I believe that God taught Adam how to sacrifice animals. This represented the shedding of blood for the atonement of sin, pointing to the ultimate sacrifice that was to come – Jesus Himself! The Bible tells us that the life is in the blood.

> *"But flesh with the life thereof, which is the blood thereof, shall ye not eat." Genesis 9:4*

> *"For the life of the flesh is in the blood, and I have given it to you upon the altar to make an atonement for your souls for it is the blood that maketh an atonement for the soul." Leviticus 17:11*

In Genesis 3:21 it says that *"God made coats of skins for Adam and Eve".*

It seems obvious to me from this verse and Leviticus 17:11 that God showed Adam how to sacrifice. And it appears to me also that He showed him how to use the skins of animals to make coats for him and his family.

Animals had to die to supply clothing, food, shelter and temporary atonement. Their skins were also used for making tents.

Through one man came sin, death and separation from God, which gave Satan control over the earth. Through Jesus Christ, sin and death were conquered; separation from God was done away with, and control of the earth was taken back from the devil.

Since you are in Christ, you are no more under the power of the devil. When you joined yourself to Jesus Christ, you reunited yourself to God. In Him are all holiness, righteousness, peace and joy, freedom, life everlasting, abundance, provision and protection.

"For as in Adam all die, even so in Christ shall all be made alive." 1 Corinthians 15:22

When men sacrificed animals to God according to the Old Testament and God accepted the sacrifices, the sins of those people were covered by the blood of the animals. And when God looked upon man, *He only saw the innocent blood of the animal and did not see the sins of man.*

The Hebrew word for atonement used in the Bible is Kaphar. Kaphar means to cover, expiate, placate, cancel, appease, cleanse, and purge.

The word atonement means to cancel, purge, appease, cleanse, expiate, placate, or do away with. Realizing this we naturally would expect the sins of the saints of the Old Testament days, to be washed away. But we must remember that the word also means to cover.

"For it is not possible that the blood of bulls and of goats should take away sins." Hebrews 10:4

The blood of the animals could not take away the sins of man but only cover them! The sacrificed animal could not do this because it was man that sinned. Only the blood of a pure and innocent man could take away sin. Thus we needed a better sacrifice than the animals. *We needed Jesus Christ!*

33

We needed a pure and sinless man, just like Adam was before his fall. That perfect, pure and sinless man was Jesus Christ. Jesus had to come and die for us.

As the animals were being sacrificed, *a life was being given for a life*.... the animals for the man's. Jesus, the pure and perfect man without spot or blemish, had to die for us. His life was given, so that we might live. *The life of a perfect sinless man for the life of sinners!*

"But with the precious blood of Christ, as a lamb without blemish and without spot." 1st Peter 1:19

~ Abraham's Bosom – Paradise ~

When the saints of the Old Testament died, they went to a place called Paradise or Abraham's Bosom. This place was beside hell but was separated from hell. It was a prison without the punishment of hell, and the devil had the keys to it.

These saints could not go to heaven then, because Jesus had not given His life for them on the cross as yet. So they waited until Jesus came for them. They were people who led holy lives unto God and sacrificed to Him in the Old Testament days.

"And it came to pass, that the beggar died, and was carried by the angels into Abraham's Bosom, the rich man also died and was buried." Luke 16:22

"And Jesus said unto him, verily I say unto thee, today shalt thou be with me in paradise." Luke 23:43

"For as Jonah was three days and three nights in the whale's belly so shall the son of man be three

days and three nights in the heart of the earth."
Matthew 12:40

*"Now that He ascended, what is it that He also
descended first into the lower parts of the earth?"
Ephesians 4:9*

When Jesus died on the cross, His body was placed
in a tomb, but His spirit went down to paradise and hell. He
went to the devil and took the keys of death and of hell
from him. He then set the people free that were in paradise
and He took them to heaven with Him. Today, anyone who
dies in Christ goes directly to heaven.

*"I am he that liveth, and was dead and behold, I am
alive for evermore, Amen, and have the keys of hell
and of death." Revelations 1:18*

*"Wherefore he saith, when he ascended up on high,
he led captivity captive (souls of paradise), and
gave gifts to man." Ephesians 4:8*

*"And the graves were opened, and many bodies of
the saints which slept rose, and came out of the
graves after his resurrection and went into the holy
city and appeared unto many." Matthew 27:52-53*

These saints were those held in paradise.
Redemption is only through Jesus Christ. He paid the
ransom price! Thus He was able to take the saints out of
paradise and into heaven with Him. His death on the cross
was the ransomed price that was paid for us all. The life of
the innocent for the condemned - us!

However, we who are in Christ are no longer
condemned.

You were redeemed by the perfect sacrifice Jesus made when He gave His life on the cross of Calvary. He allowed men to nail Him to a cross and there He died. He could have saved Himself, but He didn't. This is the reason He came.

He died on the cross, was placed in a tomb and three days later, He rose from the dead. He is alive!!

Victoriously He triumphed over the devil, defeating him once and for all. Thus, Jesus took back the power to rule the earth from the devil, after conquering sin and death.

In His life Jesus conquered sin. He was tempted by Satan, but He overcame and did not commit sin. He died, but rose again from the dead! He conquered sin and death: the two things that kept you bound to the devil. Today, you can be reunited with your Father God through new birth in Jesus Christ if you aren't already!

"Who is he that condemneth? It is Christ that died, yea rather, that is risen again, who is even at the right hand of God, who also maketh intercession for us."   *Romans 8:34*

What you need to do is to be born again: to join yourself back to God by accepting Jesus Christ as your Savior, your Lord and Redeemer.

The sacrifice that Jesus made was accepted by God the Father.

"Jesus saith unto him, I am the way, the truth and the life; no man cometh unto the Father, but by me." John 14:6

Through Adam, sin came upon us and we were separated from God. Death came upon us, and the devil began to rule the earth. But through the sacrifice that Jesus made on the cross of Calvary, we can be reunited with God and live in obedience to Him.

~ Born Again ~

How can you go to the Father through Jesus Christ?

"There was a man of the Pharisees, named Nicodemus, a ruler of the Jews. The same came to Jesus by night and said unto him, 'Rabbi, we know that thou art a teacher come from God; for no man can do these miracles that thou doest, except God be with him.' Jesus answered and said unto him, 'Verily, verily, I say unto thee, except a man be born again, he cannot see the Kingdom of God.' Nicodemus saith unto him, 'How can a man be born when he is old? Can he enter the second time into his mother's womb, and be born?' Jesus answered, 'Verily, verily, I say unto thee, except a man be born of water and of the spirit, he cannot enter into the Kingdom of God. That which is born of the flesh is flesh, and that which is born of the spirit is spirit. Marvel not that I said unto thee, ye must be born again.'" John 3:1-7

Nicodemus was a ruler of the Jews who said that Jesus had God with him. Jesus did not deny that fact. However, wanting to direct His conversation to showing Nicodemus the way to God, He told him that he *"must be born again."*

Nicodemus was a Pharisee and was very knowledgeable of the Jewish laws. Yet, he did not understand this concept of being born again. Therefore he asked Jesus what He meant by being "born again." Jesus then explained that a person must be born of water and of the Spirit to enter into the Kingdom of God.

In layman's terms, it simply means this: We have been separated from God, we have sinned, and we are going to die and go to hell. If we are not born again, if we are not reunited with God, we will spend eternity with Satan and his company in the Lake of Everlasting Fire.

When we came from our mother's womb, we were born in sin and were separated from God. But when we accept Jesus Christ as our Savior, we are reunited back to God. Jesus is the only one who saves us from the devil, sin, death and hell.

"And all things are of God, who hath reconciled us to Himself by Jesus Christ, and hath given to us the ministry of reconciliation. To wit, that God was in Christ, reconciling (redeeming) the world unto himself, not imputing their trespasses unto them, and hath committed unto us the word of reconciliation." II Corinthians 5:18-19

"For he hath made him to be sin for us, who knew no sin; that we might be made the righteousness of God in him." II Corinthians 5:21

A person is separated from God because of sin, but can be reunited with God through Jesus Christ. He died for us and rose again victoriously from the dead. Through Adam, we were joined to sin and to the devil. But through Jesus Christ we are joined to God and holiness. We need to be forgiven of our sins and to be washed in the blood of Jesus, and we need the Spirit of God living in our spirit.

"Behold I stand at the door and knock, if any man hear my voice and open the door, I will come into him and will sup with him, and he with me." Revelation 3:20

"That whosoever believeth in him should not perish but have eternal life. For God so loved the world, that he gave his only begotten son that whosoever believeth in him should not perish but have everlasting life." John 3:15-16

We are spirit beings living in a body of flesh. When we believe in Jesus Christ and accept Him as our Redeemer, His Spirit comes and lives in our spirit and we become born again. Our spirit is recreated at that very moment in the image and likeness of God. This is when we are united back to God through new birth in Christ.

If we continue to live for God, when we die, we will go to heaven and live with God forever. Or if Jesus returns first, He will take us to heaven with Him. Jesus is coming back one day soon to take His people out of this world. They will live with Him in heaven. These are those whom He finds living in obedience to Him.

What must you do to be born again?

"That if thou shalt confess with thy mouth the Lord Jesus and shalt believe in thine heart that God hath raised him from the dead, thou shalt be saved. For with the heart man believeth unto righteousness and with the mouth confession is made unto salvation." Romans 10:9-10

You simply have to believe that Jesus died and rose again from the dead. Then confess that he is your Lord and Savior. If you have not yet accepted Jesus as your Lord and Savior, just say this little prayer to God and believe it; mean every word you say:

39

Dear God: Please forgive me for every sin I have ever committed. Jesus, I accept you as my Lord and Savior. Please come and live in my spirit so that I am born again. Thank you God, for saving me. In Jesus' name I pray, Amen.

My friend, if you have said that prayer for the first time, you are born again, and on your way to heaven. Thank God! Go and confess it now! Tell someone that you are born again, that you have accepted Jesus Christ as your Lord and Savior. Jesus is now your Lord and your God.

There is a new name written down in heaven for you, in the Book of Life. It is not the name that you have now, but another name, and God knows that name. Angels are also rejoicing over you! They are ecstatic that you are saved from the grip of the devil and from hell. God bless you!

Chapter Three

Divorce
and The Operation of Satan

One generation passed to another generation and sin with it. Falling from the grace of God because of sin, Adam and Eve were separated from God spiritually. When Jesus Christ our Lord and Savior died on the cross and later rose again from the grave, the way was made for you to be reconciled to God the Father. Adam and Eve fell from the grace of God and sin was passed on from generation to generation.

Christ Jesus came and died on the cross of Calvary. He rose again from the dead, thereby making the way for us to be reconciled to God. When you became born again you were reconciled to Him. The Spirit of God entered into your spirit and resides there. You are now able to fellowship with Him. God's Spirit comes to live in your spirit and you are able to fellowship with Him as Father and child.

On this journey of life, you find that there are many obstacles, twists and turns, mountains you have to climb, and valleys you have to cross. As you continue on this passage of life, you discover that even though this Christian life is a bed of roses, there are thorns in it also.

You could call this "growing pains." However, with the help of the Holy Spirit, you are able to maneuver and to climb and cross. But there is another kind of pain that you cannot forget, and that is the kind which comes from Satan.

Satan is alive and kicking! Yes, he is your enemy, but he is a defeated enemy. He has lost the power he had to rule this earth. This is because Jesus Christ conquered him in his life, on the cross and in the grave. And now, Jesus has all power in heaven and on earth.

"All power is given unto me in heaven and earth." Matthew 28: 18

The only power Satan has today is the power that people give to him. You may question, "How?" People *give power to him* by surrendering to him and doing his bidding. And the devil will attack you every chance he gets to bring you into bondage and companionship with him. He comes against you in every way possible.

Jesus paid the price for you by His death on the cross. Through Him, you have the victory over Satan! And you have the capability in Christ to rule and reign with Him on this earth. Although Jesus is always with you, there are things that the devil comes against you with. You have to overcome and conquer in order to go on. One of these things is divorce.

~ Divorce ~

Divorce has ravished this world like a plague. Its victims are greater in number than Aids or any other disease that this world has ever seen. Almost every family has in some way been affected by divorce.

What can we do about divorce? Can we stop this onslaught on mankind that Satan has so successfully used against us? Can this plague be paralyzed in its tracks?

The word divorce can be defined in many ways. Taken from the Greek word *"apolvo,"* it means to loose, release, let go, set at liberty, send away, dismiss, put away, and divorce.

When people get married, I do not believe that they think of the day that they will divorce their mate. Nor do I believe that they contemplate how they are going to do it and what the consequences will be. I believe all they think of is how beautiful and how wonderful their marriage will be.

They think of how they are going to make their marriage the best in the world. They envision their children and how many they are going to have. The house will have to contain a certain number of bedrooms. It will have to be facing in just the right direction, with a porch and bay windows.

Their garden will have different kinds of flowers and roses. Perhaps they will plant a couple of cedars, one on each side of the white concrete pillars holding up the red iron gates. They think of beautiful things.

No one wants to be divorced. It is a long drawn out process which causes hurt to everyone. Divorce divides families and close friends. It brings friction and much tension amongst everyone involved.

When there is a divorce, people take sides. There is fighting among family members: parents against children, brothers against sisters, in-laws against in-laws. And the outcome is pain for everybody involved. Everyone hurts!

Regrettably, the ones that hurt the most are the children. This I know first hand.

In February of 1995, my brother and his wife were separated. My little nephew who was just about two and a half years old is very close to me. One day not long after their separation, I went to their home to visit my sister-in-law and my nephew. This, I often did.

I was sitting on the couch with my little nephew in my arms in front of me. He was kneeling on the floor playing with a toy truck or car. Suddenly he asked, "Uncle, where is my Dad?"

My friends, those words tore my heart. There was no answer that I could give the little boy. I did not know what to say to him because I wasn't expecting him to ask such a question. *He wasn't even three years old.*

I just continued playing with him as if I had not heard what he had said. He did not ask again.

I thank God for the strength he gave to me that day. It kept me from crying. That little boy was hurting so much! He did not know what was happening, but he knew something was wrong. Daddy was not there!

I love that boy so much! He was hurting so terribly, but could not understand the pain. He could not comprehend the emptiness that he was feeling. And he did not know how to deal with it. This is why God hates divorce!

My brother and his wife have since been reconciled. Praise God!

Both spouses pay the price. Children suffer greatly, and both spouses pay a high cost. Remember that the parents became one flesh when they married. Right now, they are torn apart! The rib is ripped out from the body as it were, and both are bleeding. Both are hurting.

However, the one that often hurts the most is the one that the other left. They sometimes give up all hope and desire not to live any longer. They cannot bear the pain. They do not know how to make it go away. It is a constant pain that feels like your heart is going to burst. Sometimes it feels as if a little plant had been planted into your heart. It grew into a tree. And then someone suddenly ripped it out of your heart leaving a gaping hole.

Like a huge tree that was pulled up by its roots leaving a wide open hole in the ground, is what it feels like in a broken and destroyed heart.

But, there is hope, thank God!

"For the Lord, the God of Israel, saith that He hateth putting away (divorce)..." Malachi 2: 16

Now if God hates divorce and does not want divorce, and people do not want divorce, why does it happen? Who is behind it? Who causes it?

The answer is: the devil. The devil is the enemy of both man and God. He hates us as much as he hates God. Satan knows that when he hurts us he is hurting God. He knows how much God loves us and so he wants to destroy us.

~ Satan Exposed! ~

From the very day you were born and even before, Satan has been seeking your destruction. He has an army that works with him. And this army of evil spirits is set up in the air. They are set up over countries, cities and towns, over homes and families, and over individuals.

The devil's strategy is to divide and conquer.

"The thief cometh not but for to steal, and to kill, and to destroy;" John 10:10

"For we wrestle not against flesh and blood, but against principalities, against powers, against the rulers of the darkness of this world, against

spiritual   wickedness   in   high   places."
Ephesians 6:12

Friends, your fight is not against flesh. It is not a battle in opposition to people! It is not against your husband or your wife. It is in opposition to the devil!

He is the one that is causing you pain. He is the one who has stolen your joy and your peace. He is the one who has robbed you of your spouse and perhaps your children. You must fight him for what he has stolen from you. He is a thief!

The strategy of the devil is to divide and conquer. He divides families, close friends and relatives, husbands and wives, business partners, churches and church members. The list goes on.

Destruction through division is his number-one objective and end result among collective bodies. Once he has accomplished this result, he works towards the destruction of the individual.

To bring about this result, he uses every means possible. He will work through the five senses of man. He will operate through the people closest to you. He will even use you.

To do this he works through the mind. He will send thoughts to your mind and tempt you to sin. He will try to give you negative thoughts of those close to you, making you think the worse of them. He will attempt to fill your mind with all kinds of garbage until you give in and commit sin. He will try to plant fear, anxiety, worry, doubt, and more in your mind. And he will continue until he has accomplished destruction, if successful.

That is why you need to guard your mind. You need to have your mind renewed with the word of God. Once the devil has your mind, he has you.

When Satan has you under his control, he attempts to cause you to do things to bring separation and divorce, division and destruction. He will cause husbands to leave wives, and wives to leave husbands.

We are spiritual beings living in a fleshly body, and our mind controls our body.

Before you do anything, you will think about it first. Your mind says to you, "you need a cup of coffee." You contemplate the thought. If you decide yes, you will go and make some or buy some, whatever the case may be. Before you drink it, your mind tells your hand to pick up the cup and put it to your mouth and drink.

So your mind controls your body. It tells you what to do. Satan will get to you through your mind if you allow him.

"This I say therefore, and testify in the Lord, that ye henceforth walk not as other gentiles, in the vanity of their mind. Having the understanding darkened, being alienated, from the life of God through the ignorance that is in them, because of the blindness of their heart (mind)." Ephesians 4:17-18

We see in Ephesians that these people lived according to the vanity of their minds. They did not know the life of God because their understanding was darkened and their hearts (minds) were blinded. The one who darkened their understanding and blinded their minds is the devil.

Whatever is in the mind of man will come out in his words or his actions. Knowing this, the devil attacks the

47

minds of people with evil thoughts. He tries to bring them under his control. *He knows that if he can control your thoughts he can control you.*

> *"O generation of vipers how come ye being evil, speak good things? For out of the abundance of the heart the mouth speaketh. A good man out of the good treasure of his heart bringeth forth good things and an evil man out of the evil treasure bringeth forth evil things." Matthew 12:34-35*

So in order for the devil to control someone, he must first have control of that person's mind. The "heart" in the books of Ephesians & Matthew, is the mind, not the physical heart of man. We think with our mind, not our physical heart.

> *"Ye are of your father the devil, and the lusts of your father ye will do. He was a murderer from the beginning, and abode not in the truth because there is no truth in him. When he speaketh a lie, he speaketh of his own, for he is a liar, and the father of it." John 8:44*

Jesus tells us plainly in the book of John who the devil is and what he does. The devil is a liar and he deceives men. He does not lie to God because he cannot trick God. He might try to lie to God, but he cannot get away with it. Read Matthew 4:1 to 11 and you will see how the devil tried to lie to Jesus, and failed. He sought to use the natural need of man to tempt Jesus. He attempted to twist the truth, but he failed miserably.

Satan's method is to send thoughts to your mind or use other people to influence your mind to encourage you to do things. Likewise he uses your senses, your sight, touch, taste, smell and your hearing - just like he did with Eve.

And your senses send all the messages to your mind. Once he has your mind, he has you. Thus he will have control to do as he pleases.

The Bible says that, whosoever you obey and serve, *his* servant you become. *You must not allow the devil to have your mind!*

"Know ye not, that to whom ye yield yourselves servants to obey, his servants ye are to whom ye obey; whether of sin unto death or of obedience unto righteousness?" Romans 6:16

As the devil sends thoughts to people and they obey and serve him, they become his servants. If they continue to obey and serve Satan without repenting and turning to God, they become bound by the devil and are controlled by him.

Whatever they are tempted with: whether it is sexual lust, fornication, alcohol, drugs, stealing, and so on, they are now in bondage to it. They are then easily controlled by the enemy. He presses the button and they jump. They are like robots which can without difficulty, be manipulated by their manufacturer.

Such people need to be set free from the devil. They need our prayers. They are like a dog on a leash being led to and fro. They are like a blind man who is led by another. The enemy lies to a person, deceives them, and blinds them, and in so doing controls them.

Some people give in to Satan's temptations and deceptions to the point of being possessed by him. This means that an evil spirit or evil spirits from the devil enters into that person and take possession of their lives. This happens most often when people have been involved in worshipping idols, in witchcraft and other forms of devil worship.

"And when he went forth to land, there met him out of the city a certain man, which had devils long time, and ware no clothes, neither abode in any house, but in the tombs." Luke 8: 27

This is one of many examples in scripture of demon possessed people.

Think about this. How can a person in their right mind take a knife and slash someone's throat? How can a person take a gun and cold bloodedly shoot someone to death? How can they, in their right minds?

These people do these things because they are controlled by an evil spirit. They are either controlled internally or externally.

The enemy will first lie to a person. Once that person accepts the lie to the point where the truth becomes a lie to them, he or she is deceived. They are then blinded to the truth and only see and believe the lie instead of the truth. Satan then has full control over that person. All he has to do is push the button.

As you saw earlier in Ephesians 6:12, there are evil spirits in the air, waiting to bring destruction. This is an army that is set up over countries, cities, towns, homes, continents and individuals.

There are different kinds of evil spirits and they do different duties.

"For God hath not given us the spirit of fear, but of power, and of love and of a sound mind." II Timothy 1:7

Fear is a spirit and it comes from the devil. Fear kills. It causes heart attacks, ulcers and other sicknesses that destroy man. Just as there is a spirit of fear there is an evil spirit for every evil thing. Spirits of fear, murder, rape, fornication, adultery, abuse, sexual lust, greed, separation, division, divorce, and so on.

> *"We are of God, he that knoweth God heareth us, he that is not of God heareth not us. Hereby know we the Spirit of Truth (Holy Spirit) and the Spirit of Error."*   1 John 4:6

> *"Now the Spirit (Holy Spirit) speaketh expressly, that in the latter times some shall depart from the faith, giving heed to seducing spirits and doctrines of devils."* 1st Timothy 4:1

You can see clearly that there are many different evil spirits that you fight against. These are the culprits; the devil and his armies which are set up in the air. *People are victims*!

When the enemy has control over a person, he gets them to do what he wants until he brings division, separation, divorce and other forms of destruction.

So Satan's strategy is to gain control of people's minds and cause them to do things they otherwise would not do. In so doing, he brings division and destruction. The enemy desires to fill your mind with his evil ways. This way it is possible for him to get you to act like him, and do what he would want you to do.

Can you imagine your mind full of the devil? Can you picture yourself full of his thoughts, full of hate, pride, malice, bitterness, unforgiveness, and so on?

Do not allow him to have control over your mind!

Chapter Four

Take Back Stolen Property

Throughout the ages, Christians have been harassed and bombarded by the enemy from every side. He has brought all kinds of sicknesses and diseases against people. He has brought poverty and other curses. And he has stolen people's peace, joy, their happiness, their finances, and more.

Thank God that you have been set free through Jesus Christ your Lord and Savior! He has given you *the power* to take back what Satan has stolen!

> *"But He was wounded for our transgressions, He was bruised for our iniquities, the chastisement of our peace was upon Him, and with His stripes we are healed." Isaiah 53:5*

> *"Who His own self bared our sins in His own body on the tree, that we, being dead to sins, should live unto righteousness, by whose stripes ye were healed." 1ˢᵗ Peter 2:24*

Jesus took your sins with him to the cross and left them there at Calvary. When you are forgiven by God, He does not remember your sins anymore. You are set free from every curse and the Lord provided healing for you also.

The last words that Jesus said on the cross were, "It is finished." He did it all at Calvary.

"Christ hath redeemed us from the curse of the law, being made a curse for us: for it is written, "Cursed is everyone that hangeth on a tree (cross)." Galatians 3:13

"For ye know the grace of our Lord Jesus Christ, that, though He was rich, yet for your sakes He became poor, that ye through His poverty might be rich." 2nd Corinthians 8:9

When he went to the cross, Jesus took with Him every sin, present and future, and every curse. And that is where He left them! This includes poverty, sickness, disease, lack, shame, guilt, condemnation, low self-esteem, inferiority, and so on. He carried your burdens to the cross, and your heavy load, and He left them there.

You do not have to carry burdens anymore. You do not have to be ashamed of your past, or feel guilty and condemned. It is behind you, over and done with. You do not have to accept sickness and disease from Satan. You are healed by the stripes of Jesus.

When the lashes tore Jesus' flesh off His body; when they spat on Him and plucked His beard and mocked Him; when they pierced His side, He bore them all for you. You do not have to bear any of these things any longer!

When Jesus was on the cross, He was there because of you. He went there to do away with everything that the devil had put on you. He had gone there to pay a price for your sins that you can never and will never be able to pay.

Christ Jesus paid the price for you in full and He ransomed you from the hands of your enemy, Satan.

Jesus paid the total price for your sins in full! You are free from every curse because you are part of the Body of Christ. You have been made one with Him through the new birth.

~ The Body of Christ ~

The *Body of Christ* is also known as the *church.* It is not the actual physical building, but the people. We are known as the body of Christ, because we became one with Him when we received Jesus as our Lord and Savior.

Jesus represented you and me on the cross. He died in your stead and mine. You should have died on the cross for your sins! I should have died on the cross for my sins! But we didn't, Jesus did.

Someone had to pay the price for sin. *"The wages of sin is death."* Jesus Christ paid that price in its totality.

Since Jesus Christ paid the price on the cross already, do you have to pay for it all over again? Why do you have to pay by being sick? Why do you have to pay by living in poverty, in shame, in guilt or in condemnation? Do you accept what the devil is trying to put on you? Why?

You must not accept what he is trying to put on you! You have to fight the enemy with all that you have and in every way that you can. *You have power* over him in the Name of Jesus!

The Bible says that you are more than conquerors in Christ Jesus - you are victorious!

"Ye are of God, little children, and have overcome them; because greater is He that is in you, than he that is in the world." 1ˢᵗ John 9:4

"Who is he that overcometh the world? But he that believeth that Jesus is the Son of God" 1ˢᵗ John 5:5

You are an overcomer because you have been born again: Jesus is living in you, and you have received mercy from God and are His chosen generation.

"But ye are a chosen generation, a royal priesthood, an holy nation, a peculiar people; that ye should show forth the praises of Him who hath called you out of darkness into His marvelous light." 1ˢᵗ Peter 2:9

Jesus Christ, who is in you, is greater than the devil who is in the world. This makes you a conqueror and an overcomer.

You are one of those who are of God's chosen generation. You are of His royal priesthood, you are of His holy nation, and you are one of His peculiar people. You are specially chosen and are of priesthood. You are peculiar and you are holy!

Why is this so? Why did He choose us to be His chosen generation, a royal priesthood, a holy nation and a peculiar people?

To show forth His praises, that is why!

What praises?

Praises of His mercy, His forgiveness, and the cleansing power of His blood; His healing, His blessings, His deliverance, and His righteousness; His peace that passes all understanding, His joy which is your strength, and His work that is being done in your life daily, changing you from glory to glory.

Your life should be a praise unto Him, a thank offering unto Him. Every day should be a day to tell about the great things He is doing in your life.

Praise the Lord and do your best in fighting the good fight against Satan. You do your best and God will do the rest. Thank him for making a way for you. Daily, praise him for the very breath you breathe.

There is so much to thank the Lord for! There is power in thanksgiving. Practice giving thanks each and every day and you will experience the difference it will make in your life.

"The thief cometh not but for to steal, and to kill and to destroy: I (Jesus) am come that they might have life, and that they might have it more abundantly." John 10:10

That's right! Satan is the thief and has stolen from people. When he divides a family and the husband leaves or the wife leaves, what happens? He has stolen from that family. He has stolen the father or mother away from their children. He has stolen that husband or wife.

He has stolen their joy, their peace, their happiness, their security, and their love. If it is your family, then you know what I am talking about. If it is your family from whom the devil has stolen, then you can *take back what rightfully belongs to you.*

~ The Family ~

The Body of Christ is parallel with the family. Before the Church existed as a Body, the family was already in existence and God had ordained proper structure in the home.

"Wives submit yourselves unto your own husbands, as unto the Lord. For the husband is the head of the wife, even as Christ is the head of the Church, and He is the Saviour of the body." Ephesians 5:21 - 23

The Church is the body of Christ and He is the Head over it. Likewise a husband is the head of his home, given that authority by God. God gave the husband to be the head of his home. *He did not give this headship to Satan.* A husband should take his rightful place in the home under God! With all submission to God, he should rule his home. This is the will of God.

Read Ephesians 5:21 to 23.

"The wife hath not power of her own body, but the husband and likewise also the husband hath not power of his own body, but the wife." 1st Corinthians 7:4

The man and his wife became one flesh and because of this they belong together. *God gave them power over each other's body.* The wife does not own her body, but her husband does. And likewise, the husband does not own his

58

body, but his wife does. *They are each other's property, not the devil's property or any body else's property!*

Whenever there is separation, a wife has every right to pray for her husband to return home because of this ownership. Likewise a husband has every right to pray for his wife to return home. Since they are each other's property, if a spouse is committing adultery, then he or she is giving away property that does not belong to him or her.

The other spouse therefore, has every right to pray the other one out of that situation and adulterous relationship that he or she is in. He or she also has the right to pray for the other to return home.

God stands by one hundred percent with the spouse who is praying, because the Lord will not go against His word. The Bible says that God hates divorce. He says for husbands and wives not to rob one another of each other's body.

> *"Defraud (rob) ye not one the other, except it be with consent for a time, that ye may give yourselves to fasting and prayer; and come together again, that Satan tempt you not for your incontinency."*
> *1st Corinthians 7:5*

The same way that spouses belong to one another, children are also possessions and gifts from God. If Satan causes them to run away from home, or if he has them bound to alcohol, sexual immorality or any other thing, as parents, you have the power of God and His backing to pray your children.

You can pray for their deliverance and for them to return home. You will be amazed to see what God will do when you pray in faith.

"Lo, children are an heritage of the Lord: and the fruit of the womb is his reward." Psalm 127:3

"For the unbelieving husband is sanctified by the wife, and the unbelieving wife is sanctified by the husband: else were your children unclean; but now are they holy." 1ˢᵗ Corinthians 7:14

Likewise brothers have the right to pray for brothers, sisters for sisters, brothers for sisters, sisters for brothers. Cain asked God *"Am I my brother's keeper?"*

"And the Lord said unto Cain, Where is Abel thy brother? And he said, 'I know not: Am I my brother's keeper?'" Genesis 4: 9

Yes, you are your brother's keeper. You are *responsible* for your brother. Do not allow Satan to trick you into thinking you have no right to pray for your brothers and sisters. You have every right to pray for them.

Do not stand by and watch them remain in blindness and deception! In prayer, remove the spiritual blindfolds that are covering their eyes, and cast them away. Ask God to give them spiritual sight. Set them free in the name of Jesus Christ!

Remember that Jesus paid a great price for everyone. When you speak to Satan in the name of Jesus Christ, he must obey. *Your family is yours, given to you by God. Take them back!* Demand your family from the hands of Satan.

Jesus did not die on the cross that you might live in defeat. He died to save you, so that you might have liberty. He made it possible for you to have an abundant life. Your

Lord and Savior defeated the devil so that you might live in victory.

Sure, the enemy might bring things against you and attack you from every angle, but you have the power to defeat him. Praise God! *You can take back what Satan has stolen from you!*

You do not owe the devil anything - he owes you. Therefore, with the power that Jesus has given to you, war against him and take back the property that rightfully belongs to you.

~ The Spiritual Battle ~

How do you fight an enemy you cannot see? How can you fight an enemy that can control someone from the outside via their mind? Or how can you war against one that can possess a person and cause them to do as he wills?

It is necessary to understand that your fight is not against people, but against the devil according to *Ephesians 6:12.* You must comprehend also that the strategy of the enemy is to divide and conquer. He seeks to control people and to bring them into destruction.

When you recognize that it is not people, but Satan who is your enemy, you can turn your attention to fight him and not people.

On your own, and in your own strength, you cannot overcome this enemy. You need supernatural strength. Jesus already gave that to you

Jesus Christ was sent by God the Father to the earth, to conquer the devil and to destroy his work. In His life, he overcame the devil by not succumbing to him and committing sin. Then He conquered him when He died and was resurrected from the dead.

"And Jesus came and spake unto them, saying, 'all power is given unto Me in heaven and in earth.'" Matthew 28:18

You saw earlier how the devil stole the power to rule from Adam and began to rule the earth. However, when Jesus conquered him on the cross He took back the power to rule the earth.

Jesus is the second Adam and He took back what the first Adam lost. Now if Jesus has *all power* in heaven and in earth, the devil does not have *any power* on this earth!

I know what you are saying: "How come the devil is causing so much destruction and harm? What do you mean he does not have any power?"

The only power that Satan has on this earth over people is what they give to him!

When the enemy has control over a person and comes to that place of being able to cause them to do wrong and damage to others, he has power over that person. He cannot do these things on his own, he uses people. And he gets that power over them when they surrender to him, and do what he requests.

Remember, in Genesis he used a serpent to cause the fall of mankind, and later he used Cain to kill his brother Abel.

In the book of John, Jesus said that the devil is a *liar* and the *father of lies* and that he was *a murderer* from the beginning. The devil did not commit the first murder physically, but he used Cain. Just as the serpent was responsible for its actions in Eden, so too was Cain, and so too are you. Satan uses people to do his bidding, but people are responsible for their own actions.

"Behold, I give unto you power to tread on serpents and scorpions, and over all the power of the enemy, and nothing shall by any means hurt you." Luke 10:19

The power that Jesus has, He has given to you. Christians are disciples and ambassadors of Jesus Christ. When you receive Jesus as Lord and Savior, and His Spirit comes and lives in your spirit, you receive the power that He has over the enemy.

Here in Luke, Jesus tells us that He gives us power over all the power of the enemy. *You have authority over the power that Satan has over people!* Remember that!

With the authority that you have through Jesus Christ, you can overcome the enemy. And for this reason He gave you *power, to overcome sin and the devil and set people free.*

"Ye are of God, little children and have overcome them because greater is He that is in you, than he that is in the world." 1ˢᵗ John 4:4,

Jesus Christ in you is greater than the devil in the world. In the name of Jesus Christ you have overcoming power! Praise God! You can win.

~ Your Weapon ~

Imagine that I gave you a gun, and told you to go into the woods and bring back some meat for us to eat. However, you do not know how to operate the gun. The gun is useless to you. It cannot help you. We are going to remain hungry.

"My people are destroyed for lack of knowledge." Hosea 4:6

You need knowledge. You need to know how to use the gun. You have to understand *how to use the power* that Jesus has given to you.

"And, I will give unto thee the keys of the kingdom of heaven - and whatsoever thou shalt bind on earth shall be bound in heaven, and whatsoever thou shalt loose on earth shall be loosed in heaven." Matthew 16: 14 & 19

"Keys" here means authority and power. Jesus is showing you how to use the power He has given to you. He is telling you that whatever you do in His Name on earth, it is done in heaven.

Binding and loosing is done in prayer. Satan, through the mind, has brought men and women into bondage, and these bonds have been made in the spiritual realm. Therefore they have to be broken in the spiritual realm through prayer.

Everywhere we turn people are bound by Satan in some way or other and it is our job to set them free in the name of Jesus Christ.

"And ought not this woman, being a daughter of Abraham, whom Satan hath bound, lo, these eighteen years, be loosed from this bond on the Sabbath day?" Luke 13:16

People can also be in *bondage* to sickness. Who had the woman in bondage? Satan did! She was in oppression to the sickness for eighteen years. And on a Sabbath day, Jesus healed her! Jesus set her free from the hold that Satan had on her.

You likewise, should be setting victims free from the devil in Christ's Name.

"And, behold, there was a woman which had a spirit of infirmity eighteen years, and was bowed together, and could in no wise lift up herself. And when Jesus saw her, He called her to Him, and said unto her, woman, thou art loosed from thine infirmity." Luke 13:11, 12

She was bound. She was in bondage. She was, as it were, chained to this sickness for eighteen years. It was a *spirit of infirmity* that oppressed her and kept her sick! The woman was under bondage not by the sickness, but by the *evil spirit of infirmity* that governed that sickness.

Your fight is not against people, but against these spirits that keep men and women under their control. This woman was bound by a spirit of infirmity and Jesus loosed her from it. He set her free.

You can do the same thing today! You have the power in Jesus to do it. You are an ambassador of Christ.

"And these signs shall follow them that believe; in my name shall they cast out devils..." John 14:12,

"Verily, verily, I say unto you, he that believeth on Me, the works that I do shall he do also - and greater works than these shall he do because I go unto my Father." Mark 16:17

Let us put a few things in perspective before we go on:

(a) The devil is a thief and has stolen from us.
(b) Jesus has given us power in His Name to defeat Satan.
(c) The devil is powerless over us as long as we do not give him place in our lives.
(d) We must not allow him to have control in any area of our lives.
(e) Jesus defeated the devil totally at Calvary!

You must take back what the devil has stolen from you. It does not belong to him! It is yours. Take it back!

~ How to overcome your Enemy ~

At this point, I am taking for granted that you have accepted Jesus as your Lord and Savior, and that you are living your life in obedience to Him. Without Jesus you cannot defeat the enemy, and without Jesus you are helpless against him.

"For we wrestle not against flesh and blood, but against principalities, against powers, against the rulers of the darkness of this world, against spiritual wickedness in high places." Ephesians 6:12

"Wherein in time past ye walked according to the course of this world, according to the prince of the

*power of the air, the spirit that now worketh in the
children of disobedience." Ephesians 2:2*

The devil's armies of evil spirits are set up in the
air. They have different ranks and different duties. They are
set up over countries and governments, over cities and
towns, over families and homes, and over churches and
individuals. And the devil rules these spirits from hell.

You have nothing to be afraid of, because you have
power over them. Evil spirits must obey you when you
command them in the name of Jesus. You are washed in the
blood of Jesus Christ and covered with the blood of Jesus.
Christ has also given His Angels charge over you to keep
you.

The first thing you must do is determine what evil
spirit is at work in the situation. Seek the Lord and ask Him
for wisdom. Find out from Him whether it is a spirit of
division, separation or divorce; a spirit of fear, anxiety or
worry; a spirit of pride, or selfishness or lust, and so on.

Identify your enemy!

If you are praying for your spouse, then you will
most likely know what spirit has him or her in bondage.
You should ask the Lord however, and He will make it
clear to you.

There are times when evil spirits are operating in a
person's life, but you are not aware of them. You are not
sure what they are. Seek the Lord! Once you have done that
and have the answer, pray for that person with the authority
that Christ has given you.

If your husband has left you and has gotten himself
into another relationship, you will pray this way:

*I come against the spirits of sexual lust, fornication,
selfishness, seduction, separation, division and*

67

divorce, and I bind them in the Name of Jesus Christ. I break their power over my husband and I loose him and set him free from these spirits, in Jesus' name. I break the relationship that my husband is having with that other person and I command it to die.

I now commit my husband into the hands of the Holy Spirit and I pray, Lord, that You allow conviction to come upon my husband's heart and give him repentance, that he may give his life to you. I pray, Lord, that you cause my husband to long for me and want to come back home to his family. In Jesus' Name I pray, Amen.

You need to be specific, that is why you pray against these spirits individually. You have to *bind their powers first* and *then loose* the person that is in bondage. After that, commit the person into the hands of God so that He may bring them home.

One thing you must seek is that your spouse should accept Jesus Christ as Lord and Savior. This should be done while he is planning to return home. Because if he returns the same way as he left and there is no change, then there is the strong possibility that he will leave again.

However, that does not mean that he will definitely leave again because he is not saved. If he returns home without giving his life to Jesus, ask him to go to see a Christian counselor with you. Go to see a pastor of a Christian church; but please, at this time, seek help from a Christian counselor or pastor. Ask the Lord to guide you to the right place.

You need to know how to love and forgive. You and your spouse need to learn how to work with each other to build a strong, loving relationship together.

The main focus of this book is to show you how to pray them home. I cannot, in this one book, show you all that you need to know. What I am trying to do in this book is to show you the power and authority you have in Christ.

My desire is that you know how to use the authority you have in Him to set the captives free, to break bondages, to bring reconciliation and healing in your marriage. In His grace and strength anything is possible. Just trust Him and believe in your miracle. You *can* defeat Satan, and you *can* have the victory!

Another thing you need to understand is that there is power in unity. If you have other Christians believing the same way as you do, and praying together with you, you will have greater results. The key is, believing together.

"Again I say unto you, that if two of you shall agree on earth as touching anything that they shall ask, it shall be done for them of my father which is in heaven." Matthew 18:19

The army we fight against is the devil and his evil spirits, not people; not your husband, not your wife, nor your children. When we come against this enemy, the whole host of heaven is with us. God and His angels fight with us. Jesus casts out devils by the power of God, and in the Name of Jesus you can do the same.

"But if I cast out devils by the Spirit of God, then the Kingdom of God is come unto you. Or else how can one enter into a strong man's house, and spoil his goods, except he first bind the strong man (devil)? and then he will spoil his house." Matthew 12:28-29

The strong man is the devil and the house he is occupying is the person over whom he has control, the person he invaded and from whom he stole. Jesus is showing you that you must first bind the devil before you can take back the property he stole.

Nothing belongs to Satan! He stole from God and man. And God took us back from him. Now we must take back from Satan what he has stolen from us. We have the power to do this, in Jesus' name.

When you pray, you must pray believing that what you are requesting you are going to have. You must have faith. Just believe! When you do your part, God does His. And your part is to pray. God's role is to answer and give you what you are asking for according to His will.

What is His will? It is what is written in scripture!

"Call unto me, and I will answer thee, and shew thee great and mighty things, which thou knowest not." Jeremiah 33:3

God always answers you when you pray and believe, when you expect to receive what you ask for. All you have to do is *believe and expect* to receive. *Your faith in Him brings the answer!*

"Therefore I say unto you, what things soever ye desire, when ye pray, believe that ye receive them, and ye shall have them." Mark 11:24

So, believe that you already have what you are asking for. God loves you more than anyone does and He wants the best for you. You are His child! He is your Father!

"Ask, and it shall be given you, seek, and ye shall find, knock, and it shall be opened unto you. For every one that asketh receiveth, and he that seeketh

findeth, and to him that knocketh it shall be opened. Or what man is there of you, whom if his son ask bread, will he give him a stone? Or if he asks for a fish, will he give him a serpent? If ye then, being evil, know how to give good gifts unto your children, how much more shall your Father which is in heaven give good things to them that ask Him." Matthew 7:7-11

"But without faith it is impossible to please him, for, he that cometh to God must believe that he is and that He is a rewarder of them that diligently seek Him." Hebrews 11:6

"Praying in FAITH moves God's hands to meet needs."

God, your Father, will give you good things when you ask Him. So, go right ahead and ask Him.

~The Authority You Have ~

There are three things I want you to understand at this time. When you bind a spirit in the name of Jesus Christ, it is bound. It does not interfere with that person any more, because you have commanded it not to! There are others that will come against that person, and so you have to continue to pray for them.

You see, Christ gave you authority that He Himself backs up. Do you believe that if Jesus told a demon to leave a person and never return, it will return? Exactly! It will not. Similarly, when you tell them to go in Christ's name, they have to obey.

"For he said unto him, Come out of the man, thou unclean spirit. And he besought him much that he (Jesus) would not send them away out of the country." Mark 5:8 & 10

Devils prefer certain places because they have more liberty to operate. This is usually because of people's ignorance. They move freely from place to place and, yes, from person to person.

If Jesus had told them to leave the country, they had to go and could not come back. This is the power and authority that Jesus has. It is the same authority that we ourselves have in Jesus' name.

"When the unclean spirit is gone out of a man, he walketh through dry places, seeking rest; and finding none, he saith, I will return unto my house whence I came out. And when he cometh, he findeth it swept and garnished. Then goeth he, and taketh to him seven other spirits more wicked than himself, and they enter in, and dwell there, and the last state of that man is worse than the first." Luke 11:24-26

This illustration shows us that demons go out and come back into a person as they wish. *This is a person whom they have possessed.* Jesus did not say it was the spirit that was cast out. But, He said that it was the spirit that went out of its own accord.

If he was cast out, he could not have said, "I am returning to my house," because it would not have been his house any longer.

"Then goeth he, and taketh with himself seven other spirits more wicked than himself, and they enter in and dwell there, and the last state of that man is

worse than the first. Even so shall it be also unto this wicked generation." Matthew 12:45

This is also the condition of any backslider.

You have power in Jesus' name to cast all devils; otherwise known as demons, out of people and also to send demons out of your country.

Now, do not go looking for demons in every person. Not every person that is controlled by an evil spirit is possessed. Most are controlled through their minds. Let me give you another example of Jesus' power in casting out devils.

"For he had commanded the unclean spirit to come out of the man."

"And they (demons) besought him that he would not command them to go out into the deep." Luke 8: 29 & 31

The New Testament was written in Greek and the word for deep is "abussos" which means "bottomless pit". This is where certain demons are bound with chains and are guarded by angels. Read - Revelations 20: 3 and 9: 1-11

Jesus had power to send evil spirits to the bottomless pit while He was on this earth. He also has that power now.

The second thing that I want you to understand is that God gave every person a "free will," or freedom to choose. However, when a person is controlled by the devil, their free will is not operating at one hundred percent.

Every person has free will to do as they please; they were given this by God. But, when they are lied to by the devil, deceived and blinded by him, they lose control to

73

him. They are not totally operating in their own free will any longer. They become confused, frustrated, and blinded. They begin to make wrong choices and decisions.

The *freedom of choice* is no longer being used to their benefit. It is used by the devil for his benefit because they are in bondage to him.

Please do not get me wrong. Every person is and will be accountable to God for his or her own action. But, have you ever had a bad habit? Perhaps drinking, taking drugs or smoking, or watching pornography, or gambling, or whatever?

You are told it is not good for you, that it gives you cancer, and that it is going to make you a pauper. People informed you that it is even going to kill you.

Deep inside of you, you know what you are doing is wrong. Yet, you are drawn and driven to do that thing with such force that you do it anyway. There comes such a burning desire on the inside of you to act out what you are feeling that you go ahead and do it anyway. Later, you cry over it and regret it.

This is how it is to be held in bondage by the devil. You do not have control any more.

"For the good that I would, I do not: but the evil which I would not, that I do. Now if I do that I would not, it is no more I that do it, but sin that dwelleth in me. I find then a law, that, when I would do good, evil is present with me. For I delight in the law of God after the inward man. But I see another law in my members, warring against the law of my mind, and bringing me into captivity to the law of sin which is in my members. O wretched man that I am! Who shall deliver me from the body of this death?" Romans 7: 19-24

Sometimes all clear thinking goes and you can concentrate on nothing else, but that burning desire. Your mind is filled up with the thoughts and the desires to which the devil has you bound. That craving controls you, it drives you, steering you wherever it will.

A person's free will is not in operation at one hundred percent at that time. They need our prayers. They are being controlled and steered like a horse with a bit in its mouth.

Let us imagine for a minute that you were blindfolded in your own home. You were then spun around a few times and told to find the front door. It is almost impossible for you to find it after that, isn't it? With all the chairs, tables, and other obstacles in the way, it would take you a very long time to find the front door. But, if someone took you by the hand and led you to the door, you would be able to find it easily.

This is what happens when the devil lies to a person, deceives them, blinds them, and in so doing controls them. He then leads them wherever he wills.

He will first lie to a person. After that person accepts the lie, the devil will continue to feed him that lie until he does not see the truth anymore. He comes to the place where he only believes the lie and does not recognize the truth for truth. He has become deceived and blinded.

Some people just do not know what the truth is, and the Bible says that *knowing the truth will set you free.* There are those who know the truth, but are so controlled that they do wrong anyway.

We need to bind the devil, loose the person, and remove the blindfold that they might see to find the door.

The third thing I want you to know is, that when a person is possessed, some demons do not go out easily, but only if we fast and pray.

"Howbeit this kind goeth not out but by prayer and fasting." Matthew 17:21

Read - *Isaiah 58 verses 6 to 11*. Do not wait until you are confronted with such a situation. Pray continually and fast often that you might be prepared.

Take back what was stolen from you! Do not give up! Fight back.

Chapter Five

Building a Solid Foundation

Relationships are not easy to develop. They take time and effort and sometimes hard work. To have a good relationship you must build on a solid foundation.

You might share your life with someone for many years, or even for just a few years. And, it will bring you closer to that person, or drive you away from them. As you spend time with people you get to know their habits, their ideas, the way they think, what they like and what they dislike. You get to know who they really are. And sometimes, you want to stay as far away as possible from them.

On the other hand, there are those that you cannot wait to go home to. They are thoughtful, kind and loving, giving and forgiving. They are easy to talk to, easy to get along with, easy to please, and they are not easily enraged or easily offended. They make you happy.

Every relationship is different. Marriage relationships are especially distinct, because every person is different. To build a strong and fulfilling relationship you need to follow the example and teachings of Jesus. You need to know how to treat other people and how to live peaceably with them.

Let us then look at some of Jesus' teachings and follow them in total obedience.

In the book of John Chapter 13, we read about the betrayal of Jesus, about the washing of the disciples' feet, and about the servant not being greater than his master. We also learn a new commandment given by Jesus.

Jesus is our example, and by washing the disciples' feet, He was teaching us how *great a love* we should have for one another.

He said that He is our Master. And if the Master washed the servant's feet, how much more should the servants wash each other's feet. If the Master loved the servants with such great love that He died for them, how much more should you and I love others of the Body of Christ similarly.

The servants, like the Master should similarly love one another. We are not greater than our Master Jesus Christ. Therefore, we ought to love one another with His kind of love.

"Verily, verily, I say unto you, the servant is not greater than his Lord; neither He that is sent is greater than He that sent Him. If ye know these things, happy are ye if ye do them. A new commandment I give unto you, that ye love one another as I have loved you, that ye love one another. By this shall all men know that ye are my disciples, if ye have love one for another." John 13: 16, 17 - 34, 35

Jesus' command was that we love one another as He loved us. We will show that we are His disciples if we love one another like He loved us.

To develop a strong relationship in a marriage, you must start with *Love*. Without love you are building on a poor foundation. Everything must be done in love: your daily interactions with one another, and your sharing together. When you are wrong or when you are right, when you are correcting or have to be corrected. And when you have to forgive or when you have to be forgiven. True love only comes from God, for God is Love.

Love is kind, it is long-suffering, and it is patient. It is not selfish, it does not lift up itself, and it is not envious. Love does not rejoice in sin, it rejoices in truth, and bears all things. It hopes for the best in all things, endures all things, and it never fails.

Read 1st Corinthians 13.

When you can love people in the way Jesus taught us, then you are on the right track and will succeed.

~ Start with Love ~

Without true love you are unable to forgive, forget or overcome. The Bible says that true love overcomes all things. Let us start by giving in love, submitting in love, praying in love, forgiving in love, teaching and correcting in love, sharing in love and talking in love. Let us do everything in love.

To love like Jesus, you need to know Jesus - not know about Him, but know Him. You need to have Him change you from the inside out, renewing you daily. You need to allow Him to transform the outer person to look like the inner you, who was made into the image and likeness of Christ.

The family and the Church are parallel. The Church is not the *building* that houses the people that go to Church, but *it is the people who* go to Church. We are the Body of Christ and He is our Head. He is our Leader and we follow Him.

> *"For as we have many members in one body... So we, being many, are one body in Christ and every one member is one of another." Ephesians 1:22-23,*

> *"And hath put all things under His feet, and gave Him to be head over all things to the church. Which is His body, the fullness of Him, that filleth all in all." Romans 12:4, 5*

Ephesians 5 talks about *"The Analogy of family and church."*

> *"...Submitting yourselves to one another in the fear of God. Wives, submit yourselves unto your own husbands, as unto the Lord. For the husband is the head of the wife, even as Christ is the head of the church: and he is the saviour of the body. Therefore as the church is subject unto Christ, so let the wives be to their own husbands in everything. Husbands, love your wives, even as Christ also loved the church, and gave himself for it: That he might sanctify and cleanse it with the washing of water by the word, that he might present it to himself a glorious church, not having spot, or wrinkle, or any such thing; but that it should be holy and without blemish. So ought men to love their own wives as their own bodies. He that loveth his wife loveth himself" Ephesians 5:21-28*

Obedience to this two-part instruction is the only way to truly have a successful and happy marriage relationship. The wife is to have an attitude of love and a heart of submission, and the husband is to have an attitude of love.

~ Nurture ~

As Jesus Christ is the Head of the Church, likewise the husband is the head of his wife and his home. He has been made the head of his wife by God himself.

Jesus is our Head and as the Head, He leads us and guides us: He provides for us and protects us; He nourishes us and strengthens us. He is our Shepherd and has placed under-shepherds, or pastors to overlook His flock: the Church.

Jesus uses pastors to teach us His Word and His commandments. They feed us by preaching the Word of God to us. You see, your spirit needs food just like your physical body needs food, and the food on which your spirit feeds, is the Word of God.

Scripture tells us that *"In the beginning, was the Word, and the Word was with God, and the Word was God"* John 1: 1

The word of God is as important to us for nourishment, as the food we eat.

"All scripture is given by inspiration of God, and is profitable for doctrine, for reproof, for correction, for instruction in righteousness; that the man of God may be perfect, furnished unto all good works." 2nd Timothy 3: 16, 17

After you have received the Word of God into your spirit, the Holy Spirit takes that Word and renews you with

81

it. He transforms your character and attitude. Holy Spirit causes you through the word of God to think like Jesus, speak like Him and act like Him. He uses it to change the outer you daily, since your spirit which is the inner you was already transformed. It was recreated at your new birth.

You have to remember that when you became born again, your spirit was changed into the likeness and image of Christ. You became one with Him. You became a new person. The soul and flesh area continues to be transformed by Holy Spirit on a daily basis.

"I am crucified with Christ: nevertheless I live; yet not I, but Christ liveth in me..." Galatians 2:20

"Therefore if any man is in Christ, he is a new creature: old things are passed away; behold, all things are become new." 2nd Corinthians 5:17

~ Responsibilities of Husbands~

"Husbands, love your wives as Christ also loved the church, and gave Himself for it." Ephesians 5:25

A man's duty and responsibility is to love his wife to the point where he would give his life for her if necessary. Not that he would commit suicide, but that he should be able to say, *"take my life and let my wife live."* This is the kind of love God wants us to have for one another.

"Greater love hath no man than this, that a man lay down his life for his friends." John 15:13

A man's wife is greater than his friend. She is more than a friend to him; she is his companion for life, she is his flesh and blood, his very body. His love for her must be greater than he has for any other friend. *The greatest is love*. Love conquers all.

Because the husband is the head of the wife, he has an important job to do. *He is commanded to love his wife like Jesus loves the Church.* But, part of his duty is also to "wash" his wife and the rest of his family with the Word of God. He is responsible to nurture them with scripture.

"That he might sanctify and cleanse it with the washing of water by the word. That he might present it to himself a glorious church not having spot, or wrinkle, or any such thing, but that it should be holy and without blemish." Ephesians 5:26-27

The same way, in which Jesus has set pastors over the Church, He has set the husband over the family. He is the head of his own family under Christ. Therefore, the responsibility of husbands is similar to a pastor. Together he and his family have a pastor; the pastor of their local church.

Since he was made the head of the home by the Lord, he is therefore required to nurture his family with the Word of God.

When a man does not fully understand his headship, or obey God's instructions in this regard, a terrible burden falls upon the wife's shoulders. Likewise, a woman who fails to understand the importance of her role and her submission to her husband, hinders his headship over her in Christ. This opens the door to the enemy to operate in their lives.

Husbands, your wife is your flesh and blood, you have become one flesh with her. One flesh; not two, but one! She is your flesh, your blood, and your body. When you love your wife the way you are commanded to by the Lord, your "body" will be strong, healthy and blessed.

"So ought men to love their wives as their own bodies. He that loveth his wife loveth himself."
Ephesians 5:28

"For no man ever yet hateth his own flesh; but nourisheth and cherisheth it, even as the Lord does the church. For we are members of His body, of His flesh, and of His bones. For this cause shall a man leave his father and mother and shall be joined unto his wife, and they two shall be one flesh."
Ephesians 5:29-31

Think of your wife for a moment: her hair is yours, her beautiful eyes are yours, her lips are yours, her entire body is yours. From the crown of her head to the soles of her feet, all are yours. She is yours!

You love your hair, don't you? You love your body, don't you? You love your eyes, your nose and your lips, don't you? She is your body! *Love her!*

Would you let someone poke your eyes out for a million dollars? I don't think so.

Your eyes are precious to you. You would not want to give up this beautiful gift of sight. Not to behold beauty any longer; not to see green trees or the birds flying from their branches any more, is not a comforting thought.

To not be able to see beautiful sceneries any more; to not be able to see people again; to only hear them and guess what they look like; forever being unable to see a beautiful smile on a baby's face, how tragic, that would be!

Surely, you do not want to give up this precious gift! I am sure you love and cherish your gift of sight. Your wife is such a gift! She is precious and she is yours; all yours. And you are hers. Love her! Cherish her.

A husband belongs totally to his wife. And a man's wife belongs totally to him. They both belong to God, not to the devil or anyone else. I encourage you husbands to love your wives in just the same way as Jesus loves you. Cherish them and nourish them, protect them and provide for them, esteem them, and you alone will enjoy true rewards from them.

~ Responsibilities of Wives~

Wife, your husband is God's gift to you. Nurture him, and submit to him as Christ commanded you. Make God the centre of your marriage this way! Love your husband. Treasure him!

> *"The wife hath not power of her own body, but the husband and likewise the husband hath not power of his own body, but the wife." 1ˢᵗ Corinthians 7: 4*

Every woman must also love her husband and respect him. He is your head and your leader under Jesus Christ our Lord. Look at the great command he was given! To love you as Jesus loves the Church and died for it - this is a great command! Your husband represents Jesus Christ and has great responsibilities concerning you. Love him as Jesus taught you.

> *"A new commandment I give unto you, that ye love one another, as I have loved you, that ye love one another. By this shall all men know that ye are my disciples, if ye have love one for another." John 13:34-35*

Dear woman, love your husband and show him respect. Always lift him up and regard him. Never put him down! Like Jesus said, *"love one another and by this you will be my disciple."*

In loving your husband you are obeying Jesus. He is also your flesh and blood, your very body. Love him and surrender to him under God in all submission. Stand by his side.

Remember that when God gave Eve to Adam, He gave her to be his help mate. She was his helper; she made Adam what he was not. He was incomplete without her. God saw that and said, "It is not good that the man be alone."

You are your husband's help mate - you make him what he isn't. Remember that!

If you are not being what you are supposed to be, your husband will not be what he is supposed to be. You make him what he isn't. You are his wife. Be his wife!

Don't be a married woman, or a child bearer, or a housewife, or whatever else people may label you. *Be his wife!* You will make him what he should be. You make him complete. You will cause him to be strong and be respected by others. Your love for him, and your respect and submission to him will cause him to stand tall. That is why God gave you to him and not to another! He will work through you to accomplish all this.

"Wives, submit yourselves unto your own husbands, as is fit in the Lord." Ephesians 3:18

Sometimes a woman can find herself in a very difficult situation. She might have a husband who abuses her physically, verbally or emotionally. And then she recognizes that the scripture commands her to submit to her husband. What is a she to do in such a situation?

The Bible tells her to submit to her husband *as is fit* in the Lord. She must submit to him in everything that is godly. If you are being abused, do not accept it, and submit to it, get help. Seek counsel from your pastor, get help, but submit to everything that is godly.

"Likewise, ye wives, be in subjection to your own husbands, that, if any obey not the word, they also may without the word be won by the conversation of the wives. While they behold your chaste conversation coupled with fear. Whose adorning let it not be that outward adorning of plaiting the hair, and of wearing of gold, or of putting on of apparel. But let it be the hidden man of the heart, in that which is not corruptible, even the ornament of a meek and quiet spirit, which is in the sight of God of great price." 1st Peter 3:1-4.

Scripture is not saying here that a woman is not to wear clothes or not to look good. The word of God is addressing the heart of a woman and encouraging that she should act with a godly attitude and character.

It is saying that a wife could win her husband over by submitting to him and obeying him. By respecting him and being faithful to him, having chaste conversations with him, using sweet words that lift up and that do not put down, she will win him.

She ought to take care of herself and look good outwardly, but most of all she should adorn her inner person with a meek and quiet spirit, a peaceful and loving spirit. The only way she can accomplish this is by obeying the Word of God.

Who can tell a woman how to be a woman? Who can teach a wife how to love her husband? Only a woman knows how to be a woman. And only a wife knows how to love her own husband.

Only a wife knows how to be a wife. So be his wife. Win your husband's trust by being truthful and honest in everything. In all things let him see your love. And never give him cause to doubt your love for him.

"And whatsoever ye do, do it heartily, as to the Lord, and not unto men. Knowing that of the Lord ye shall receive the reward of the inheritance: for ye serve the Lord Christ." Colossians 3:23-24

Whatever you do to, for, and with each other as husband and wife, whether in speech or in deed, do it with your whole heart. *Do it as if you are doing it for Jesus!* Know that you will receive your reward from Him, here and in the hereafter. Always consider each other in whatever you do.

Think of the other person before you do anything. Will your actions hurt them or bless them? Will they make him or her happy or sad? Will your actions cause them to stumble and fall, or will they cause them to be strong and have life?

Never be selfish or self-centered!

Do not think of what you can get from this relationship. Think of what you can give to it. Always put the other person first! *Jesus put us first.* He loved us before we loved Him. And because He loved us, He died that we might live. He wasn't selfish.

"Love worketh no ill to his neighbour: therefore love is the fulfilling of the law." Romans 3:10

"A new commandment I give unto you, that ye love one another, as I have loved you, that ye love one another." John 13:34

Every good and righteous act goes back to love. Love does no harm to anyone. It fulfils all the laws of God. God is love. If you want to build on a solid foundation, you must build on love!

Nothing can overcome love. True love overcomes all things. Jesus loves. He did everything in love. You are His servant and you are not greater than Him. You can be like Him in your thinking, your speech, and your actions. You can live like Him! Build on a solid foundation. *Build on love - Christ's love.*

Chapter Six

Living
In His Overcoming Power

When you became born again, your inner person: your spirit, became alive unto God. God quickened or brought to life your inner self. Before you were born again, you were dead unto God or separated from Him and on your way to hell and eternal destruction. However, because you are joined back to God through Christ you have become alive unto Him.

You are now able, by the help of the Holy Spirit, to live in obedience to God. In the past, you obeyed the devil and sinned because it was common to you. This was the result of being "a child of the devil." Today, you are a child of God.

As human beings we are made up of three parts: the spirit, the soul and the body. Our body houses the soul and spirit which is also called the inner person or inner man.

The soul is where we feel. It is our emotion, passions, desires, appetites and feelings.

The spirit is where we know and discern what is right and wrong. It is our intellect, will and conscience.

Before becoming born again you did what was common or natural to you because of the nature of Satan. Today, you are able to obey God by the help of Holy Spirit. He is the One, who caused your inner person to become alive to God. Though sin is still natural to your flesh, you are able to obey God and refrain from sin in His strength.

"There hath no temptation overtaken you but such as is common to man: but God is faithful, who will not suffer you to be tempted above that ye are able; but will with the temptation also make a way to escape, that ye may be able to bear it."
1st Corinthians 10: 13

The knowledge of sin is still recorded in your mind and is still being used by the devil to tempt you. But, becoming a Christian and having Jesus live inside of you, gives you the power in His name to overcome. As a Christian you have a lifestyle to live and a path to walk. And this standard of living is totally different from the one to which you had become accustomed.

Throughout your life you have been influenced in every way possible by your enemy, the devil. He has bombarded your mind with thoughts of wickedness of every kind. This includes sexual lusts, greed, selfishness, hate, malice, pride, rebellion, idolatry, and every evil thing you can imagine.

He has used radio and television as doors to access your mind. His evil spirits have sent thoughts to your mind throughout your life. He has used people to plant things into your mind. And he has even used our education system to teach you things contrary to God. Satan has used every means possible and is using everything he can, to try to keep you in bondage.

Now that you are a born again believer in God, you have been changed. *You have been made into the new you. Now you are a brand new creation.*

God transformed your spirit, but the soul remained the same and needs to be changed on a daily basis. Your inner self is now one with Christ, but your soul and flesh continue to change from glory to glory. This is where you come into a place where you think more like Jesus, speak more like Him, and act like Him.

Ask yourself this question: Since I became a Christian have my thought patterns changed? How about my speech: Do I still speak like the devil? Do I continue to act like a student of his?

Unless your mind has been renewed by the Word of God, you most likely think the same, speak identically to the old you, and act similarly. Likewise the temptations continue to be the same. This is because you are tempted by what is common to you, what is already in you - in your mind; the things that you already have knowledge of.

In order to live this Christian life to its fullest, overcome old thought patterns and temptations, and be victorious in every area of your life, you must change what is in your mind. Your thinking must change.

"When you change your thinking you will change your life."

Each of us must change from thinking like the devil to thinking like God!

Before the transformation of your sprit, the devil put his thoughts into your mind and you learned to think like him and live like him. At the present time, you need to put God's thoughts into your mind so that you are able to live like Him. God's thoughts include every word written in the Bible.

From this day forward you should put as much of God's Word into your mind as possible. This way you will be able to think like Him and live like Him. You are His child and as His child, people of the world should see God in you. So change your thinking.

~ The Word ~

"I beseech you therefore, brethren, by the mercies of God that ye present your bodies a living sacrifice, holy, acceptable unto God, which is your reasonable service. And be not conformed to this world, but be ye transformed by the renewing of your mind, that ye may prove what is that good, and acceptable, and perfect will of God."
Romans 12:1-2

Sometimes as a Christian, you may think that God has to do everything for you, and will do everything for you. However, this is not true. God will do His part, but you have to do yours.

He has caused you to become alive unto Him. Your part is to present yourself to Holy Spirit that He may transform your thoughts, your speech, and your actions, through the word of God. You have to initiate the renewing of your mind so that you might be transformed outwardly. Your mind must be renewed so that you can think differently and thus act differently.

If you were to read the above verses and paraphrase them they would read like this: the good and acceptable and perfect will of God is that you change your thinking into

94

godly thinking, and not go back into living the old lifestyle of the world (devil) by renewing the thoughts of your mind. This is what it really means.

The perfect will of God is that you change; that you think like Him, speak like Him, and that you act like Him. The only way you can accomplish this is by changing your thinking, as your mind is renewed by the word of God.

Think of your mind as a dirty drinking glass that you would put under a tap, and begin to fill with water. As the water flows into the glass, it flushes the dirt out of the glass making it sparkling clean.

> *"That He might sanctify and cleanse it with the washing of water by the word. That He might present it to Himself a glorious church, not having spot, or wrinkle, or any such thing, but that it should be holy and without blemish."*
> *Ephesians 5:26-27*

This portion of scripture was written to the Church in Ephesus by Paul, who paralleled the Church with the family. He was teaching husbands to "wash" their wives with the Word of God in the same way that Jesus washes the Church.

A husband, as the head of the home, is required to read the Bible to his family and wash them with the Word of God. However, each individual is responsible unto the Lord for his or her own washing.

Christianity is a personal relationship with Jesus Christ, and you have a personal requirement to build that relationship. Therefore, you must read the Bible daily putting the Word of God into your mind. Then you will grow in knowledge in Him.

"Sanctify them through thy truth, thy word is truth." John 17: 17

"Now ye are clean through the word I have spoken unto you." John 15:3

Most times a person will leave church feeling fresh and clean. This is because he is washed by the preaching of the Word of God. The word cleanses and refreshes him. As you read the Bible daily it will wash or flush your mind. Similar to water from a tap that flushes out dirt from a drinking glass, so too the word of God cleanses your thinking! The Word will flush out the thoughts of your past; the thoughts that the devil placed there.

The Word of God is a collection of the thoughts of God. As it begins to take up residence in your mind you will think like God, speak like God, act like God and accomplish the will of God.

> *"Till we all come into the unity of the faith, and of the knowledge of the son of God, unto a perfect man, unto the measure of the stature of the fullness of Christ." Ephesians 4:13*

> *"In the beginning was the Word, and the Word was with God, and the Word was God. And the Word was made flesh, and dwelt among us. The Son of God is Jesus Christ and the knowledge of the Son of God is the Word of God." John 1:1 & 14*

~ Overcoming by the Word ~

Jesus Christ is the Word that was with God in the beginning and was made flesh and lived among us. He is God and when you put the Word of God within you by reading the Bible, you are abiding in Him and He is abiding in you. This is the area of the soul. He already resides in your spirit.

"If ye abide in me, and my words abide in you, ye shall ask what ye will, and it shall be done unto you." John 15:7

If you live in Jesus and continue to have His Word abide in you, you will overcome. This is because whatever you ask Him then, will be according to His word, and He will do it for you.

> *"And to know the love of Christ, which passeth knowledge, that we might be filled with all the fullness of God." Ephesians 3:19*

> *"But speaking the truth in love, may grow up into Him in all things, which is the head, even Christ!" Ephesians 4:15*

> *"That ye put off concerning the former conversation the old man, which is corrupt according to the deceitful lusts. And be renewed in the spirit of your mind. And that ye put on the new man, which after God is created in righteousness and true holiness." Ephesians 4:22-24*

By taking time to read the Bible you will know the Love of Christ. Not only will you know His love by experiencing it in your everyday personal relationship with Him, you will also grow in knowledge of Him through His word. You will also learn to speak the truth and put away lies.

You will grow up in God, maturing into a strong and stable child of His. Your conversation will change because of what you are putting into your mind; truth and holiness. You will be taking in Christ Himself.

Grow in God by renewing your mind. Put away your old ways and put on the ways of God. You could be successful in every area of your life if you were to mature in God on a daily basis. You would think like God, act like God, speak like God, and accomplish like God. This does not make you God, but you are a child of God, and He is your Father.

"I am the vine, ye are the branches, he that abideth in me, and I in him, the same bringeth forth much fruit, for without me ye can do nothing." John 15:5

"If ye abide in me, and my words abide in you, ye shall ask what ye will, and it shall be done unto you." John 15:7

Jesus is the vine, and if you live in Him and His Word lives in you, you can ask what you want and you will have it. This is because you will be thinking like Jesus, and will therefore ask for exactly what He wants you to have. You will be speaking His Word and asking according to His word.

The secret is to live in Him. If you live in Jesus and He lives in you, you will bring forth much fruit, just like a branch that continues to live in the vine.

Jesus was the Word spoken when God said, "Let there be light", and Jesus is also every word written in the Bible. The more of the Word of God you take in, the more like Jesus you will become in character and attitude. The Word will wash your mind of all the things the devil has placed there and wants to continue to put there. It will change your thinking and it will help you to live in obedience to God.

"But be ye doers of the word, and not hearers only." James 1:22

The Word will take the place of whatever evil was in your mind. It will strengthen your faith and will give you hope. It will put the thoughts of Christ in your soul. *It will help you to obey God.*

> *"For the word of God is quick, and powerful, and sharper than any two edged sword, piercing even to the dividing asunder of soul, and spirit, and of the joints and marrow, and is a discerner of the thoughts and intents of the heart." Hebrews 4:12*

The Word of God is powerful and is able to separate even your soul from your spirit, and know the thoughts and intentions of your mind. Thus, the Word is able to make your mind clean and your thoughts holy. You must wash your mind daily in the Word of God. It is food for your spirit and nourishment for your soul.

> *"But He answered and said, it is written, Man shall not live by bread alone, but by every word that proceedeth out of the mouth of God." Matthew 4:4*

You cannot live without food, can you? Likewise, you cannot live without the Word of God. Man shall not live by bread alone, but by every word of God. The Word will strengthen you and renew you. It will make you a healthy Christian.

It will help your communication with God by showing you what God expects from you and what you can ask for. You will know how to live and how to act towards others.

You will learn more of how the devil works, and you will recognize when he is speaking to you. This is because when you know what the Bible says, and you hear something said to you that is contrary to the Bible, you will realize that it is not God speaking to you, but Satan.

~ Knowledge is Power ~

As you gain more knowledge of God you become more powerful in Him. You will live more and more in victory. It is going to be harder for the devil to lie to you. And you will live an abundant and full life.

"My people are destroyed for lack of knowledge." Hosea 4:6

Because of the knowledge gained by reading the Bible you will not be destroyed. Therefore renew your mind. Strive to be more like Jesus in your thoughts, words and actions. Allow Christ to take you on a daily walk through His Word. You will be the beneficiary of the great result.

The bottom line is this: you can be born again and have Jesus living on the inside of you. You can have all the power that Jesus has given to you. But, if you are not living in Him, and if you do not have His Word living in your heart, you will live a defeated life.

When you look at your life, all you will see is failure. Living in Jesus Christ and having His Word living in you -*John 15:7,* is putting His Word into your mind daily and living in obedience to that Word.

We live in a very dark world, a very evil world. It is a world that can swallow a person up into its darkness like a vacuum. Like quicksand swallowing up its unsuspecting victim, so too, this world can devour the unknowing soul. Suddenly, you realize how far away you have gone from God, and how deep you are in sin. You could conform to the world and turn back to doing evil.

You cannot afford to let this happen to you. That is why you need to be transformed daily in your soul area. You must make yourself aware of how transformation happens and you must do your part. God will do His part, but you must do yours.

This is why you need to wash your mind daily, putting on the fullness of Jesus, growing up into Him. As you do that, you will become more like Him in your thinking, speaking and acting. You will then shine as brightly as a bonfire in a dark night. The world will see *"Christ in you the hope of glory."*

You are going to walk the right path and not walk into quicksand. You will live victoriously. You will see your way before you and not stumble. You are going to march on with gladness and joy, and full of the peace of God.

You must focus on what is ahead of you: an eternal promise; living with Jesus for all eternity. No more sorrow, no more pain, no more tears, no more suffering, but joy and peace for eternity. To live in Jesus' overcoming power is to have Him saturate your being with Himself

~ Praises ~

Another way of living in the overcoming power of God is to live in His Presence.

"But thou art holy, O Thou that inhabitest the praises of Israel." Psalm 22:3

God Himself lives in the praises of His people. He comes and overshadows you like a cloud, hovering over you as you praise Him. This is when you sense His presence in a strong way. You feel His peace, His comfort and His love. You know that He is there.

King David understood this and wrote about it. When David was a shepherd boy, he cared for his father's sheep alone in the fields and sang praises to God. Daily he fellowshipped with the Lord and the presence of the Lord was surely with him. The Lord lives in your praises.

You can sing praises to God and you can also speak praises to Him. Praising God is thanking Him, telling Him you appreciate Him for the things He has done. It is being grateful for the miracles He has worked, for the healings, the blessings He has bestowed upon you, and the love He has shown to you in so many ways.

When you praise God before people, you are lifting Him up that all might see how good and awesome He is. In the same way, as you praise Him when you are alone and in your private prayer time, He comes and over-shadows you with His presence. As your songs of praise or your words of praise ascend to Him, His presence descends upon you and stays with you. As long as you live in an attitude of praise and gratitude, you experience His presence in a greater way.

~ Worship ~

Worshipping Him also brings His presence. Worshipping God is being grateful to Him for His forgiveness, His grace, His love, and all that He has done for us. Worshipping Him means loving Him, thanking Him, and bowing down in adoration before Him. It is pouring your soul out to Him in love. It is different, and intimately deeper than praise.

Praise is done in an attitude of gratitude and thanksgiving, joy and merriment. It is celebratory. Worship is more of a surrendering to God your Father, acknowledging Him for who He is, and appreciating Him. Worshipping is giving to Him; giving of your money, your time, and most of all, giving Him yourself.

Worshipping God is one to one. It is a relationship so intimate and close it is not easily broken. It is an experience of being lost in the presence of Almighty God, your Father.

Where the presence of the Lord is, there is no power on earth that is greater. The presence of the Lord brings deliverance, healing, joy, peace, comfort, love, compassion, miracles and blessings. All that is of God comes with His Presence. *Where the presence of the Lord is, the devil is exposed and he does not stay.*

In Old Testament days the presence of the Lord was in the Ark of the Covenant. God had instructed Israel to build an Ark and had told the people that His presence would be in this Ark.

He also gave them specific instructions about carrying the Ark. They could not touch it with their hands, and some died whilst attempting to do that. But, whenever the Ark was among His people there were blessings and all that is written above.

Read all of 2nd Samuel Chapter 6.

> *"And the ark of the Lord continued in the house of Obededom the Gitite three months, and the Lord blessed Obededom, and all his household."*
> *2nd Samuel 6:11*

Obededom had the presence of Almighty God in his house. You can also experience blessings from God like Obededom. You need to be in His presence on a daily basis. You need to have His presence in your home.

The presence of the Lord will drive your enemies out from you.

"Behold the ark of the covenant of the Lord of all the earth passeth over before you into Jordan. And as they that bare the ark were come unto Jordan, and the feet of the priests that bare the ark were dipped in the brim of the water, (for Jordan overfloweth all his banks all the time of harvest). That the waters which came down from above stood and rose up an heap very far from the city of Adam, that is beside Zaretan, and those that came down toward the sea of the plain, even the salt sea, failed, and were cut off, and the people passed over right against Jericho." Joshua 3:11, 15, 16

God had told Joshua that He would be with him and magnify him before the people. As Joshua obeyed the Lord and the Priests entered the water, God stopped the water of the river from flowing down. His people crossed over into the land that He had promised them.

As soon as the Ark with the presence of the Lord was in the water, the miracle happened. The water stopped flowing down and gathered in one place, and the children of Israel crossed the Jordan. They went in and possessed their promised land.

The presence of the Lord in the Ark removed the obstacle from the path of the Israelites. In the same way, the presence of the Lord in your life will remove Satan from before you. The result will be that you will enjoy all the blessings of God. So discipline yourself to praise and worship God every day and pray to Him, communicating your requests and needs.

~ Fasting ~

Fasting is also worship. Fasting helps to break down your flesh and bring it into subjection to your spirit. You spirit is in subjection to Holy Spirit. Thus you need to bring your flesh into surrender to Holy Spirit who resides in your spirit.

> *"Is not this the fast that I have chosen? to loose the bands of wickedness, to undo the heavy burdens, and to let the oppressed go free, and that ye break every yoke? Is it not to deal thy bread to the hungry, and that thou bring the poor that are cast out to thy house? when thou seeth the naked, that thou cover him, and that thou hide not thy self from thine own flesh? Then shall thy light break forth as the morning, and thine health shall spring forth speedily, and thy righteousness shall go before thee; the glory of the Lord shall be thy reward. Then shalt thou call, and the Lord shall answer; thou shalt cry, and he shall say, here I am. If thou take away from the midst of thee the yoke, the putting forth of the finger, and speaking vanity. And if thou draw out thy soul to the hungry, and satisfy the afflicted soul; then shall thy light rise in obscurity, and thy darkness be as the noonday .And the Lord shall guide thee continually, and satisfy thy soul in drought, and make fat thy bones, and thou shalt be like a watered garden, and like a spring of water, whose waters fail not." Isaiah 58:6-11*

Fasting is not only abstinence from food. It is also taking from what you have and giving to those who are in need. It is feeding the hungry with bread that you would have eaten. It is sharing what you have; the blessings that the Lord has bestowed upon you. After all, everything that you possess was given to you by God!

Fasting is also sharing or giving shelter to those that do not have. It is clothing the naked; those who do not have enough clothing to cover their bodies.

This is all part of fasting, and it is a continual thing. This is not to be done only once or twice. Fasting breaks the bands of wickedness, and it takes heavy burdens away from people. It sets them free from oppression.

When you have done all this, you will receive your reward: the rich presence of God which will come and cover you. You will call and the Lord will answer you and bless you. You are going to be healthy and shine brightly for the Lord. Your soul will be satisfied. Blessings will continue to flow to you from God, and your well will not run dry.

"But as for me, when they were sick, my clothing was sackcloth: I humbled my soul with fasting." Psalm 35:13

"When I wept, and chastened my soul with fasting, that was to my reproach." Psalm 69:10

Fasting humbles you and it brings your soul, through chastening, to obedience and faith in God. Therefore, fasting is another form of worship to God. You need to fast! This helps bring your flesh into subjection to God.

"Howbeit this kind goeth not out but by prayer and fasting." Matthew 17:21

Jesus said these words after His disciples could not cast out a demon from a boy. He told them that kind of spirit would only go out by fasting and prayer. Could it be then, that if they had fasted they would have been able to cast out the demon? Yes, I believe so.

Do not wait to come face to face with a situation and then decide to fast. Start now! Build your relationship with Almighty God now. In so doing you will be able to overcome in every area of your life.

Remember, where the presence of the Lord is, *the devil does not stay.* Get your life saturated with the presence of God and *nothing* will be able to stand in your way to victory! God will work through you to bring triumph. Do your part, He will do His.

~ Prayer ~

"Praying always with all prayer and supplication in the Spirit, and watching thereunto with all perseverance and supplication for all saints." Ephesians 6: 18

"I thank my God upon every remembrance of you, always in every prayer of mine for you all making request with joy." Philippians 1: 3, 4

"Be careful for nothing, but in everything by prayer and supplication with thanksgiving let your requests be made known to God." Philippians 4: 6

As you read the Word daily, putting the thoughts of God into your mind, as you praise and worship God daily, and as you fast, do not forget to pray.

Prayer reaches the heart of God and He is willing, able, and waiting to answer your prayers. You should pray every day, communicating your requests and your needs to

Him. Bring the needs of others also before Him, and thank Him for the answers.

When the answers to your prayers are manifested, you will have more for which to praise Him. You will testify before God's people of His goodness, mercies, forgiveness, grace, protection and provision.

"Be sober, be vigilant; because your adversary the devil, as a roaring lion, walketh about, seeking whom he may devour." 1ˢᵗ Peter 5:8

"Submit yourselves therefore to God. Resist the devil, and he will flee from you. Draw nigh to God, and He will draw nigh to you." James 4:7-8

Satan will always seek opportunities to tempt you and bring destruction upon you. Be awake then, and aware of his doings, and when he tempts you resist him and he *will flee* from you. Therefore, submit yourself to God, surrender your whole life to Him, and resist Satan.

The devil will have no choice but to flee from you. You have power in Jesus' Name to command him to stop tempting you and to leave you alone. He *has* to obey you or answer to Jesus Christ Himself!

A bird might fly over your head many times, but it will not make a nest in your hair if you do not allow it. *Do not allow the devil to build a nest of temptations in your mind.*

When the temptations come to your mind, resist them. Do not dwell on them, and do not think about them. Command the devil to leave you and set your mind to think on the things of God.

"Wherefore take unto you the whole armour of God, that ye may be able to withstand in the evil day, and having done all, to stand." Ephesians 6:13

When you have done everything, stand in the victory of God. Do your best and God will do the rest.

~ Fellowship ~

All the above things you must do, but very importantly you must not forget to fellowship with other believers in an evangelical church. Fellowship is important because it brings us together as one body.

It is in the church setting that you will experience the presence of Holy Spirit in a more powerful way. This is where you as a believer, gather together with one mind with other Christians to worship Jesus. And in this union the presence of Holy Spirit is felt and experienced in a greater way.

The church setting also, is where you have opportunities to share the love of Jesus Christ for others, and accept them as your family. Other Christians are part of Christ's Body therefore they are part of you.

The common fellowship with other believers is the place where you will also grow in the word of God. We worship and praise Jesus Christ in unity and with one voice in the church gathering. And it is here, that we pray for one another and find comfort in each other's friendship.

Fellowship between you and other believers, will be strengthened by their encouragement and friendship. So find a church where the word of God is preached, and where Christ is lifted up through Holy Spirit. When you find that place, let the fellowship and teaching there point you closer to your heavenly father. Thank God for it, and begin to fellowship there on a regular basis. Submit to the Leadership of the church and grow in the Lord.

> "If there be therefore any consolation in Christ, if any comfort of love, if any fellowship of the Spirit, if any bowels of mercies, fulfill ye my joy, that ye be like-minded, having the same love, being of one accord, of one mind. Let nothing be done through strife or vain glory; but in lowliness of mind let each esteem others better than themselves... Let this mind be in you, which was also in Christ Jesus." Philippians 2: 1- 5

> "Let us hold fast the profession of our faith without wavering: (for He is faithful that promised;) and let us consider one another to provoke unto love and to good works: not forsaking the assembling of ourselves together." Hebrews 10: 23 - 25,

Christianity is a growing process; it is a lifestyle. Having and living a *personal relationship* with Jesus Christ is what it is all about. If you do not develop this personal relationship, you will not excel in your Christian walk.

Without this *personal relationship* with God you will remain stagnant; you will remain in one position. You may be born again, having new life in Christ, but still have a shallow relationship Him: not communicating with Him; not sharing with Him; not depending on Him.

This lack of intimate relationship can be compared with a marriage that is "on the rocks." The married couple live in the same house, eat at the same table, may sleep in the same bed, but do not have intimate relationship with each other. They slowly drift apart.

They do not communicate, they do not do things together, they just do not share too much of anything with one another. They will remain like stagnant water. And you know that stagnant water stinks! You do not want that for your life.

So develop and build a strong relationship with Jesus by reading His Word, praising and worshipping Him, fasting as you would plan, and pray every day. When you constantly communicate with Him and learn to know His voice and obey Him, you will live victoriously in His overcoming power.

Live, therefore, in the overcoming power of God - *Start today!*

Chapter Seven

What Now?

How often do you stop and look at your life, and wonder about where you are in life? How often do you say to yourself, "How far have I come? What is holding me back? Why can't I overcome this situation? Why am I so frustrated and confused? Why don't things work out my way?

Most often you might ask the latter question of why things do not work out your way. Things do not work our way because our ways are not God's ways, and when we try to do everything our way and in our strength, we fail most of the time.

What we fail to do is consider and ask ourselves, "Where am I? How far have I gone? What do I need to do to overcome this situation?"

We need to ask ourselves questions like these, and then we will begin to step in the right direction and overcome our situations.

Knowledge is a very powerful thing, and it can be used either for you or against you. However, when you gain knowledge and act upon what you know, you can be powerful. You can overcome any situation in your life if you have the right information or knowledge and act upon it.

Having the right information or knowledge and doing nothing with it is not wise. It is like trapping water from a river into a pond and not using it or allowing there to be a continuous flow. The water becomes stagnant and after some time it will stink.

You do not want to be like stagnant water! You want to smell fresh all the time.

When you stop and begin to ask yourself questions like these, then I believe that you will start to seek the answers. By seeking, you will gain the knowledge needed to overcome Satan and the world, and live victoriously.

You have read this book because you are seeking answers. You are seeking information and you are seeking truth.

In this book you have been given answers and you have been given truth. This is information and knowledge to make you stronger in your life. Now it is your turn! What you do from here will decide how the next step in your future come out.

We do not know all the answers and neither can we by ourselves solve every problem. But, Jesus Christ our Lord and Savior, is the answer to every problem. Seek Him in every area of your life and turn to Him with every problem.

When problems involve other people, you must understand that you cannot change people. Only God can change people and He does, every day. You must allow Him to work in people's lives as you fast and pray for them. Have the patience to wait for God to do a complete work in them.

Things do not change overnight, especially those things that have developed over a period of time. Therefore have patience and let God do His complete work.

Always rely on Holy Spirit to lead and guide you. Not only depend on Him in your everyday life, but in your prayer life and in your devotions. Rely on Him and trust Him to lead you into all truth. Learn to know His voice that you may know when He is speaking to you.

You will be able to walk in the right direction, speak the right words, and do the right things. *He is The Way, He is The Truth, and He is The Life. He has the answer to every problem - He is the answer!*

This book is meant to be a supplemental source to help you put certain truths into perspective. Read your Bible daily, and let God be the source in your life for everything. Take what is written in this book and use it to the glory of God Almighty.

Let your life shine for Jesus Christ. Let it be a bonfire that blazes with new life in Him. Allow Christ Jesus to be exalted in your life. Men and women, boys and girls will notice the difference. They will be drawn to the presence of Jesus Christ that shines from inside of you, and God will be glorified.

My utmost desire is to glorify God: that He be exalted in your life and my life and that we all may grow up into His fullness; that we may be witnesses for Him; that we may receive His reward, His glory, and His blessings.

This book was written with you, the reader, in mind. It was written that you might receive knowledge. Take that knowledge and use it in your situations everyday. Put this wisdom to use in your everyday life, overcoming and conquering to your joy and comfort, and to the glory of God.

It was written from the experience of heartache and pain, disappointments and shame. But, it was also written from experiencing victory and blessings, comfort and joy, and from being in the presence of the Lord.

Read this book over and over again, grasp the truth in it, and use it. Remember, it is up to you now. What you do with this knowledge that you have gained can only be decided by you. *Do your best - God will do the rest!*

God bless and keep you, and make His face shine upon you. The peace of the Lord that passes all understanding, and the joy of the Lord that is your strength, dwell in you richly. Let Holy Spirit comfort you and lead you in all truth. Let Him speak to you and give you wisdom, knowledge and understanding. May the Lord Jesus Christ be exalted in your life! Amen.